Companion to the ARTS OF AFRICA at the Denver Art Museum

Edited by Syokau Mutonga

Texts by Syokau Mutonga, Merikokeb Berhanu, Margaret Nagawa, and Kendall Taylor

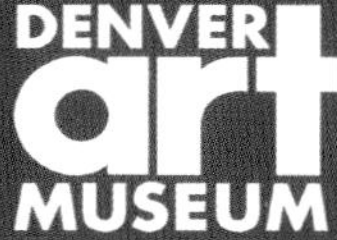

CONTENTS

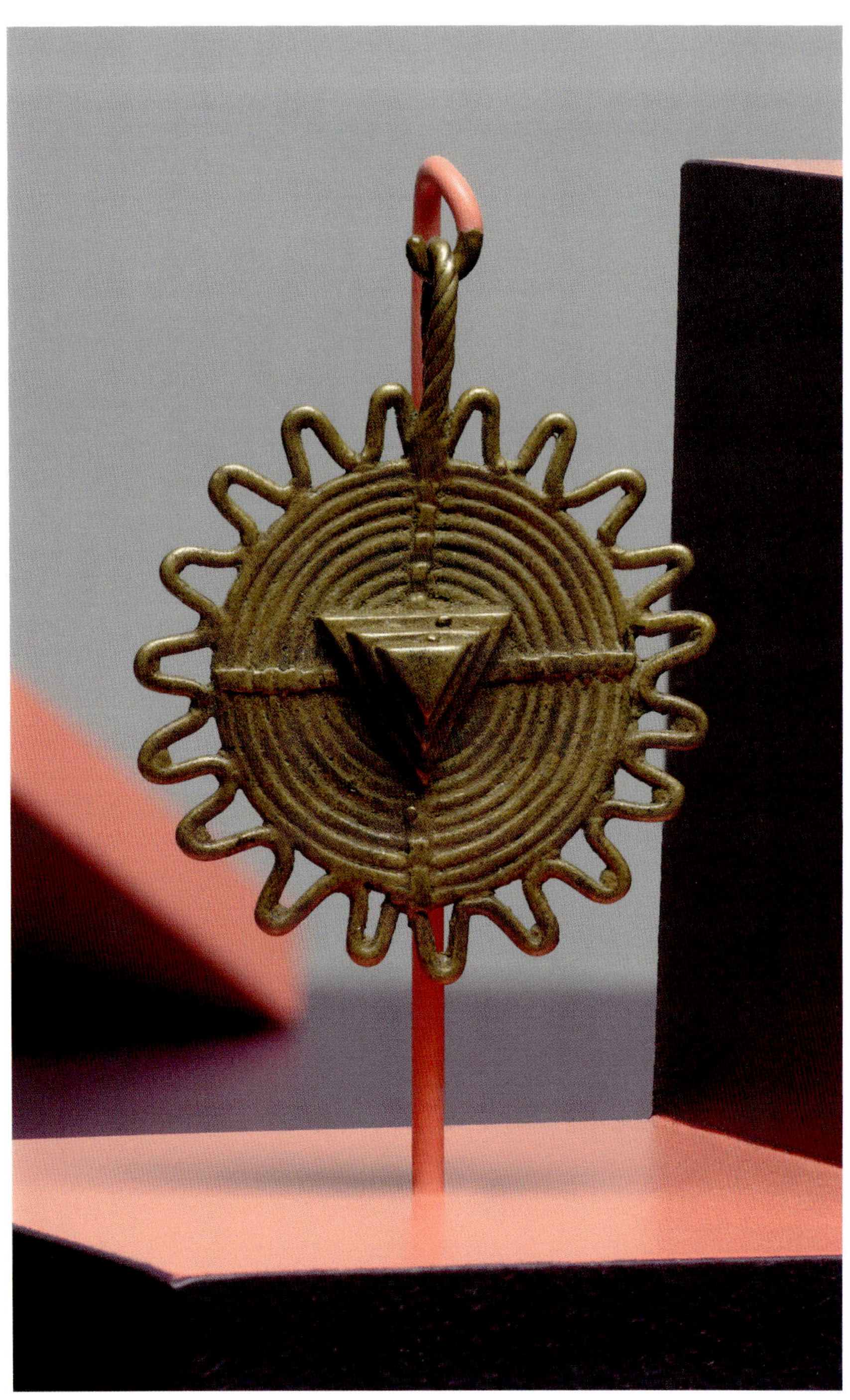

Ashanti artist. Gold Weight, early 1900s. Brass, 2¼ × 2⅛ × 1⅞ in. Native Arts acquisition funds, 1948.596.

DIRECTOR'S FOREWORD

CHRISTOPH HEINRICH
FREDERICK and JAN MAYER DIRECTOR

The arts of Africa collection at the Denver Art Museum is around seven hundred objects—small but mighty—built up over nearly a century. The museum began collecting art from Africa under the direction of Frederic Douglas, a curator of Native Arts hired in 1929. In 1999, the department hired Moyo Okediji, our first assistant curator to specialize in art of the continent, who held the position until 2008. Due to the support of the Anderman family, we have in recent years established a fellowship for arts of Africa, creating even greater opportunities for focused collecting practices and scholarship.

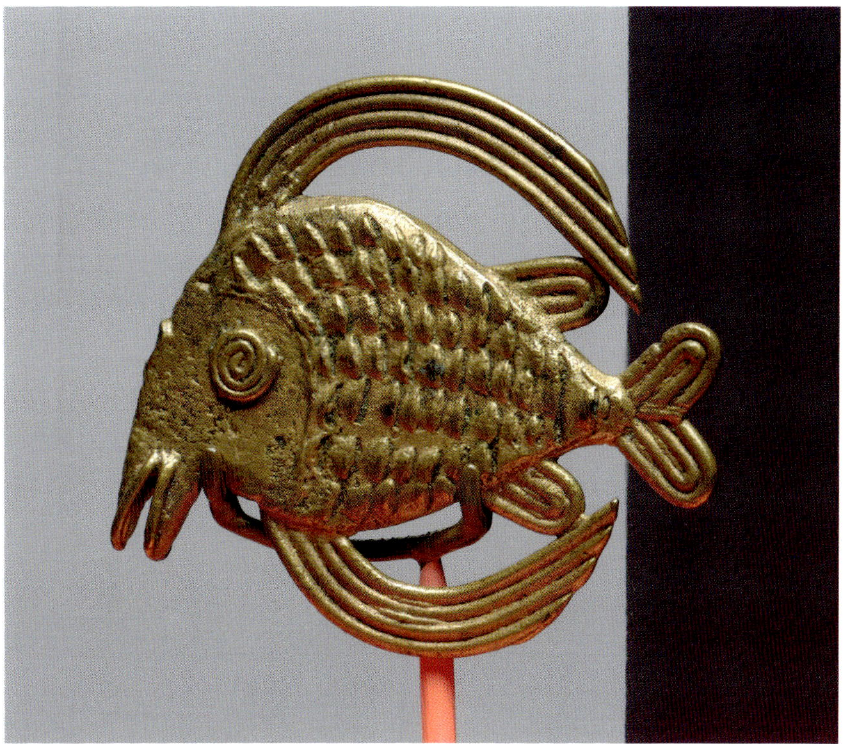

Ashanti artist. Gold Weight, early 1900s. Brass, 2¾ × ½ × 1⅛ in.
Native Arts acquisition funds, 1948.599.

With the reopening of the Hamilton Building came the reinstallation of the arts of Africa collection and the chance to rethink the presentation in a fresh, new way. Re-opened to the public in 2023, the gallery presented a vibrant space that celebrates art from across the continent and throughout time.

With brightly colored walls, music from Africa and the diaspora, and videos of masquerades and interviews with contemporary artists, the space is lively and inviting. The works on view span thousands of years, from ancient Egyptian carving to acquisitions from the twenty-first century. Displaying painting, printmaking, sculpture, textiles, and jewelry, the installation honors the variety of practices of African makers and related artists across the globe.

Syokau Mutonga has been the Anderman Family Fellow for Arts of Africa since 2024. I extend my gratitude to her for overseeing this comprehensive publication. Her approach to the subject is expansive and inclusive, and she thoughtfully acknowledges the complicated history of museums' involvement with colonial collecting practices. In addition to overseeing this companion guide, she assisted with the repatriation of the museum's Benin bronze plaque that was acquired in 1955. Through newly available documentation, it came to light that the work had been looted from its rightful owners, and Mutonga worked with our Provenance department to return the plaque to Nigeria's National Commission for Museums and Monuments. However, by negotiating a five-year loan back to the Denver Art Museum, the team secured a valuable means of educating our visitors here in Colorado about the object and its history.

I thank Margaret Nagawa, Kendall Taylor, and Merikokeb Berhanu for contributing their valuable voices to this publication, the Anderman family for supporting the fellowship position, and John P. Lukavic, Andrew W. Mellon Curator of Native Arts, for his reliable and visionary leadership of the department.

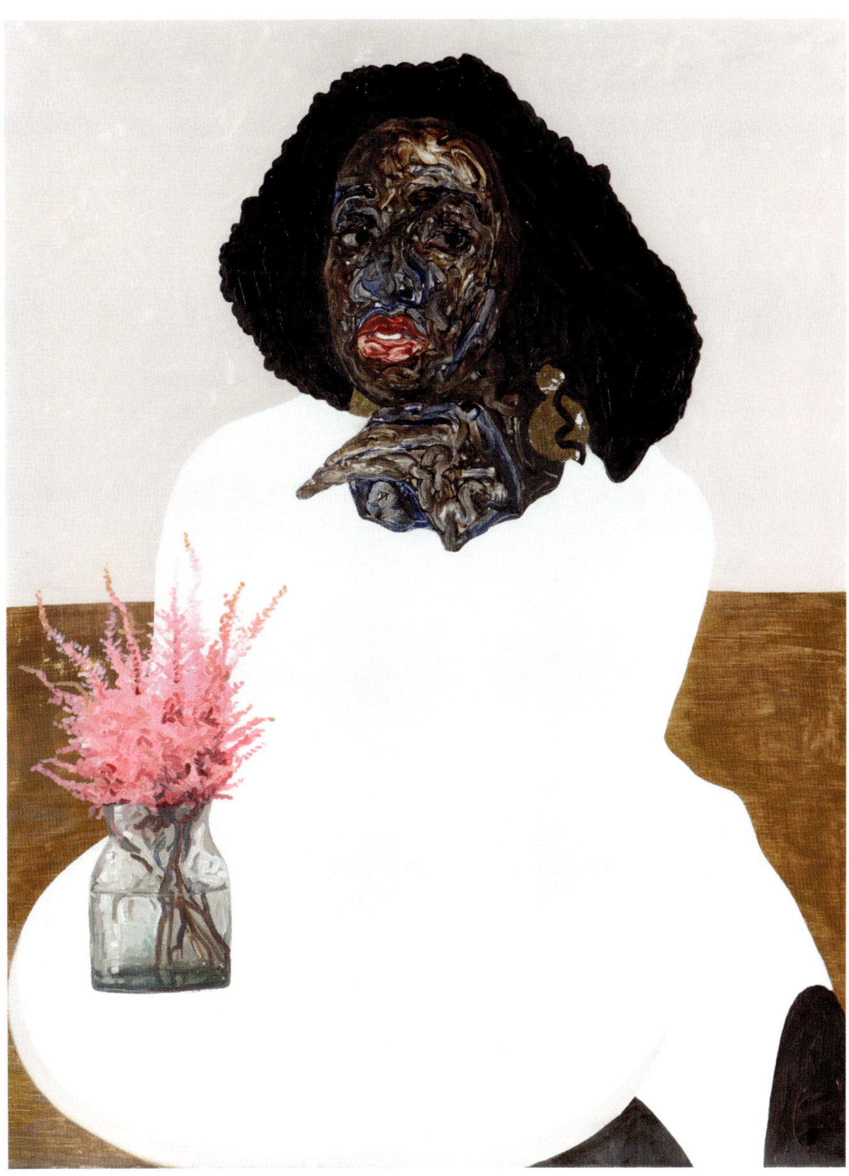

Amoako Boafo (Ghanian, born 1984). *Pink Astilbe*, 2021. Oil on canvas, 63 × 51½ in. Purchased with funds from Ralph L. and Florence R. Burgess Trust and Black Arts Collective funds from Craig Ponzio, the Art of Giving Fund–Colorado, Robin Baba-Koncilja and Nick Koncilja, Chris and Lu Law, Maude Lofton, Tina Walls, Ellen Anderman and James Donaldson, Leah Ashley, Toni and Abasi Baruti, Javon Brame, Senga Nengudi Fittz, Donna and Steve Good, James and Wendy Holmes, Philae Knight, Cleo Parker Robinson, Aaron Payne, Stephanie and Floyd Rance, and Nicole and Kyle Schneider, 2024.191.

The ARTS OF AFRICA COLLECTION
at the Denver Art Museum

SYOKAU MUTONGA

What are the arts of Africa? The arts of Africa celebrate people and cultures across vast tracts of land and endless ages of time. They are a material archive of Africa's historical and contemporary expressions from the earliest development of homo sapiens in eastern Africa's Rift Valley to today's vibrant art hubs in Dakar, Abidjan, Lagos, Addis Ababa, Nairobi, Kampala, Marrakesh, and other cities. Across their vibrant landscapes which encompass sunbaked deserts, dense tropical forests, rolling savannas, cool highlands, and jagged mountain peaks, Africans have found ways to express their religious beliefs, social customs, and life experiences through story, music, dance, sculpture, and other art forms. As African people have moved beyond the continent, willingly or not, their arts have become interwoven into broader, diverse Black geographies. Seeing the arts of Africa as part of a wider vision of Black art and expression, rather than from a fixed geographical location, frees them from being perceived as peripheral and inconsequential: They can then be defined beyond the African continent, Western exceptionalism, and art history.[1]

The arts of Africa collection at the Denver Art Museum is relatively small compared to other collections in the museum, totaling slightly over seven hundred artworks, mostly from the nineteenth and twentieth centuries. It is a collection that focuses on the diverse artistic traditions of Africa and includes rare and exquisite works in sculpture, textiles, brass, painting, printmaking, and jewelry. Although the collection is substantial in West African art, particularly Yoruba works, it also features a few masterpieces from the southern, eastern, central, and northern regions of the continent. To address the gaps in the collection, this book traces the diverse aesthetic artworks by artists from Africa and its diaspora across the museum's departments. Consequently, the art discussed spans more than the arts of Africa collection, featuring artworks from the Modern and Contemporary, Architecture and Design, Arts of Asia, Latin American Art, Western American Art, and Latin American Contemporary Art departments. This invites us to examine the broader transformations, interventions, and new forms of expression that emerge as Black people navigate the world. Such a position is taken because, while not all Black people identify as African, broadly speaking, Black worlds often draw meaning from Africa. Although a single book or museum collection cannot hope to convey the breadth and richness of African and Black cultures, past and present, we hope to weave a tapestry that celebrates these identities and cultures through art.

This book is organized chronologically, with the historical part of the book divided into three sections: the commerce and trade of the West African coast, that of the Indian Ocean coast, and combs and masks. The section on the West African Gold Coast discusses how art techniques were based on locally available resources. Gradually, the gold trade, both within and outside the continent, attracted commodities and art forms from farther afield.[2] The section on the Indian Ocean trade asks us to reconsider where Africa, Asia, and Europe begin and end. The art of this region also featured local tastes intermingled with designs from distant lands to produce unique styles. It demonstrates how these African communities were at the intersection of historical and contemporary ways of negotiating belonging in the world and exercising agency and power, highlighting the impossibility of controlling the crossings of people, ideas, and things.[3] The section on combs and masks contrasts the Western idea of "authentic" versus "inauthentic" African art with an African view of these objects.

In the second part of the book, contemporary artworks celebrate the radical acts of Black artists who have invented and reinvented themselves through their art in ways that resist erasure. They show that Black realities are rich as living archives of emancipatory transformation. They are continually straddling myriad identity margins and bridging various divides, always recognizing and submitting to the interconnections, nuances, and complexities that make up life.[4]

Commerce and Gold Trade In West and Central Africa

In the ninth and tenth centuries, traders from the Arab world traveled across the Sahara Desert searching for gold. Initially, they sought gold sourced from alluvial deposits in Bambuk (now Senegal) and Bure (now Mali). Later, they supplemented it with ore from the gold mines of the Upper Volta (now Burkina Faso). Accordingly, records of the gold trade are well documented in Arabic historical and religious sources, as well as in the few remaining gold coins in circulation from that time. For example, a Qu'ran leaf in the Denver Art Museum's collection, inscribed in gold, is believed to have been part of a Qu'ran manuscript that was originally kept in the library of the Great Mosque of Kairouan, Tunisia, since at least 1294 (cat. 1).[5]

The manuscript was unbound during the Ottoman conquest of North Africa in the sixteenth century. The earliest set of leaves, of which the museum's leaf is probably part, was then taken to Istanbul. Presently, approximately sixty-seven leaves are in Tunisia, with more than one hundred leaves of the manuscript dispersed across collections worldwide. Regrettably, because of gold's intrinsic

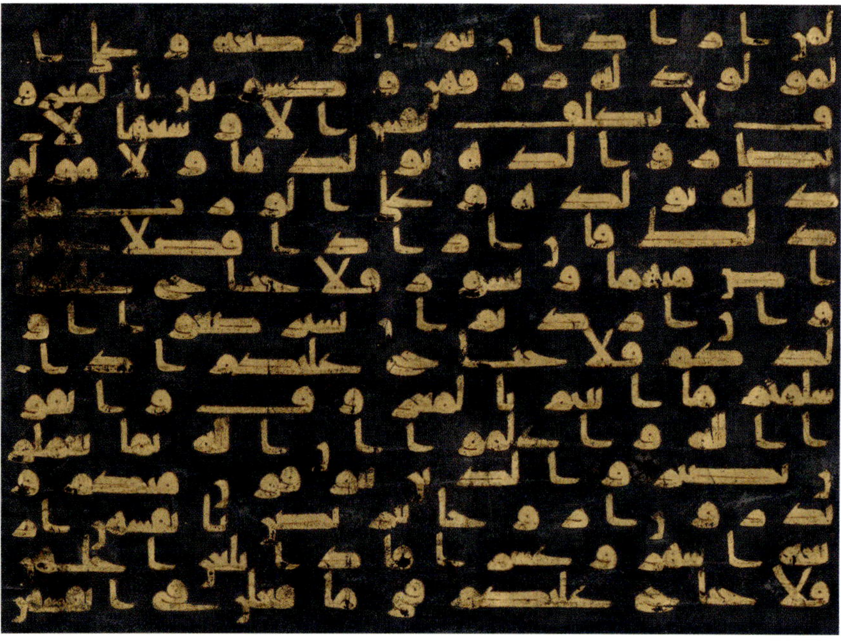

Cat. 1. Probably North African artist. Qur'an Leaf in Kufic Script, late 800s–early 900s. Gold on blue vellum, 8¾ × 12½ in. Bj Averitt Islamic Art Fund, 1999.78.

fungibility, as well as colonization, there is little evidence of the gold that circulated within Africa and from Africa to other continents. But the gold script used on this Qu'ran leaf is evidence of its widespread use at the time and the significance of West Africa's gold reserves for the rest of the world.

Furthermore, when Western Europe returned to the gold standard in 1252, Italian connections to trans-Saharan trade played a role. The cities of Florence and Venice had a privileged trading relationship with Tunis, which was then under the control of the Hafsid dynasty in North Africa, just across the Mediterranean Sea and an important hub of commerce. It enabled both Italian city-states to mint their own coinage, using gold from West Africa as the primary material.[6]

The Gold Coast

The ancient kingdom of Mali, famous for its gold trade and once the richest city in Africa, spread across parts of modern-day Mali, Senegal, the Gambia, Guinea, Niger, Nigeria, Chad, Mauritania, and Burkina Faso. Its most famous king was Mansa Musa, and he is often considered the zenith of Mali's power and prestige. He reigned between 1312 and 1337, when the Mali empire reached its peak.[7] In addition to large reserves of gold, Mali also traded in enslaved people, ivory, spices, silks, and ceramics. The Akan also participated in the gold trade in West Africa. The Akan live in the forested regions that make up modern-day Ghana, as well as parts of present-day Côte d'Ivoire and Togo. They participated in the gold trade primarily from the beginning of the fifteenth century until the end of the nineteenth century, integrating the commodity into their everyday lives. The Akan subgroups that participated in the gold trade included the Asante (also known as Ashanti), Baule, Fante, Akyem, Brong, Sefwi, Anyi, and Nzima.

Gold Weights

To regulate and control the gold trade, merchants and rulers created brass weights called *abrammuo* (singular: *mrammuo*) to establish standard units of measure. They were cast from brass using the lost-wax method: A mold was made by first sculpting a detailed original from a piece of wax, clay, or resin. This was dipped or painted with a clay slip—a liquefied clay mixture with the consistency of a cream. After the slip dried, the mold was placed in a furnace where the wax drained away. Then the mold was filled with molten brass that would solidify into the original shape.

The gold weights at the Denver Art Museum represent those from the Asante (present-day Ghana) and Baule (present-day Côte d'Ivoire) cultures.[8]

Handling gold dust was a delicate skill, usually managed by men. Most adult men owned a set of weights, often inherited from previous generations. The wealthier a man was, the more diverse his set. Because standardization was important, the sizes of the weights were fairly consistent. In cases where blacksmiths made a weight that did not accurately reflect its intended weight, small brass nodes were added to it to bring it to the correct weight (cat. 2).

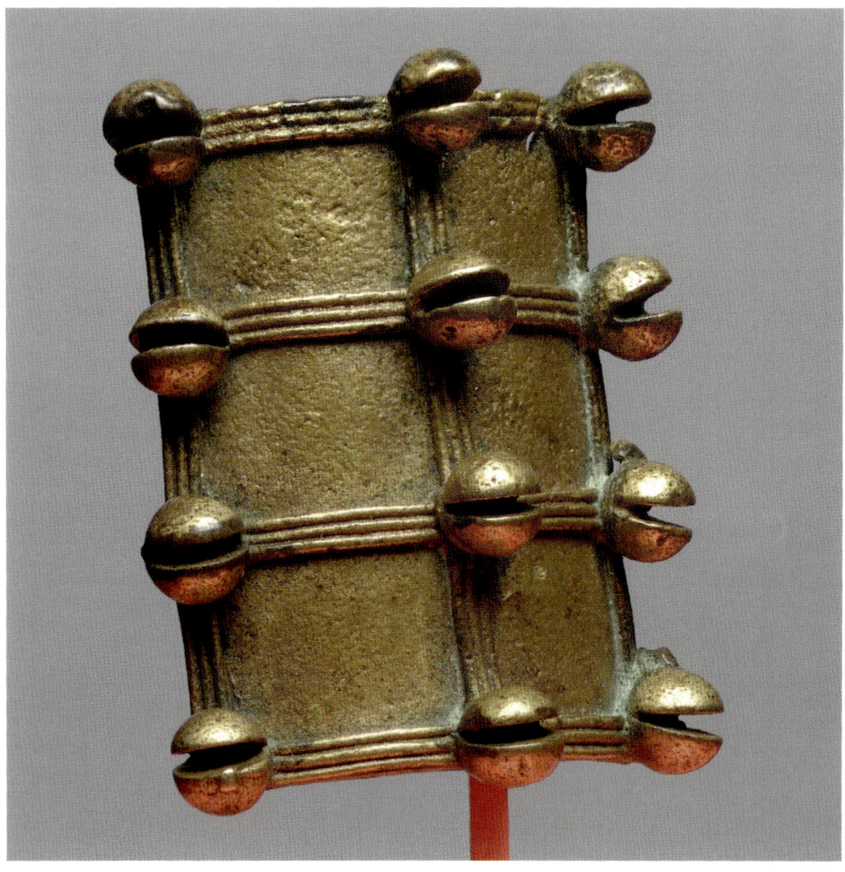

Cat. 2. Ashanti artist. Gold Weight in the Shape of an Anklet with Bells, early 1900s. Brass, 1⅞ × 1½ × ½ in. Native Arts acquisition funds, 1948.605.

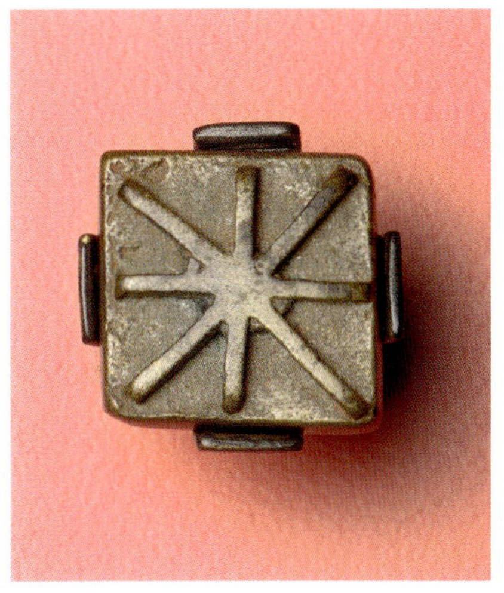

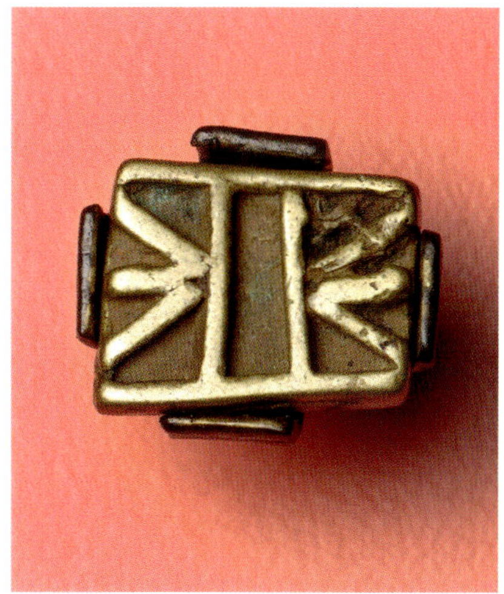

Cats. 3 (left) and 4 (right). Ashanti artists. Gold Weights, early 1900s. Brass, ⅝ × ⅝ × ⅛ in.; ⅝ × ½ × ⅛ in. Native Arts acquisition funds, 1952.654, .655.

Conducting transactions in gold was a lengthy process. The buyer and seller first agreed on the amount of gold to be exchanged for a commodity. Then the buyer would weigh the appropriate quantity of gold on his own scale, using his own weights. The scales used to weigh gold were held over the left thumb with the palm turned upward, reducing the chance of interference from the rest of the hand.[9] The seller would then use his own scales and weights to remeasure the buyer's gold. Concluding the transaction was not easy because the buyer often disagreed with the gold measures and had to restart the process.[10]

Dating the evolution of gold weights over time is mostly speculative because gold weights have not been excavated in archaeological contexts. It is generally believed that the abstract and geometric designs are the earliest weights, possibly dating to the sixth century, influenced by the Islamic culture of the first trans-Saharan traders. Islamic art avoids representations of divine beings because of the religion's prohibition of idolatry. Many of the design motifs used in the geometric gold weights are also found in Akan textiles and on other decorations in the home. Some of these design motifs are called Adinkra, visual symbols that represent concepts, proverbs, and aphorisms in Akan culture. Two weights in particular (cats. 3 and 4) feature an Adinkra symbol called Ananse Ntentan (spider's web), a symbol of wisdom, craftiness, creativity, and the

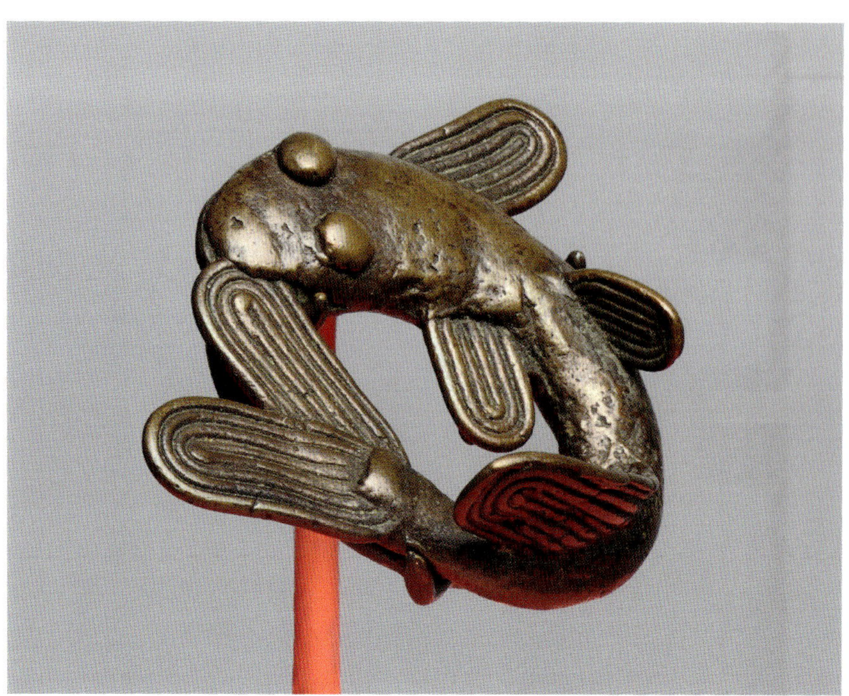

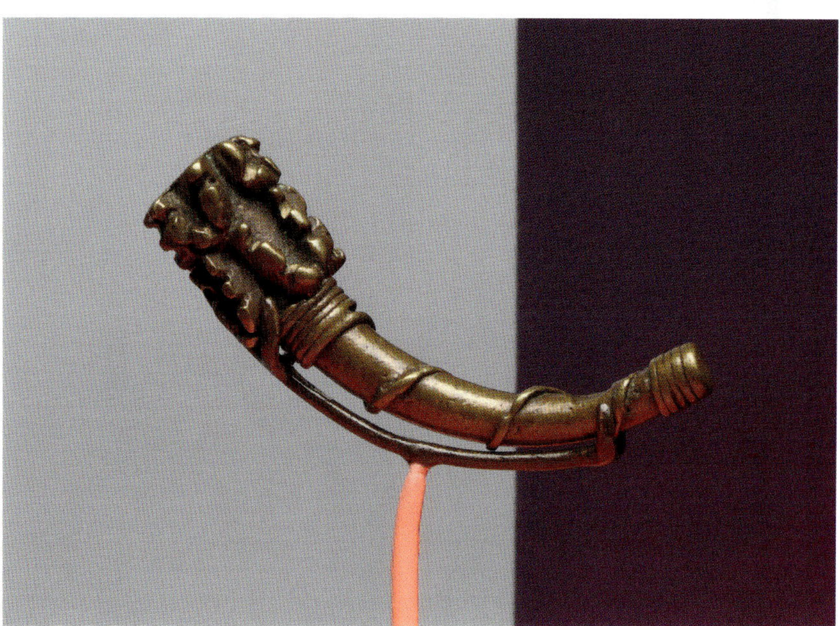

Top: Ashanti artist. Fish-Shaped Gold Weight, early 1900s. Brass, 1¼ × 1¼ × 4⅜ in. Native Arts acquisition funds, 1949.4174.

Above: Ashanti artist. Elephant Tusk–Shaped Gold Weight, early 1900s. Brass, ½ × ½ × 2¾ in. Native Arts acquisition funds, 1948.598.

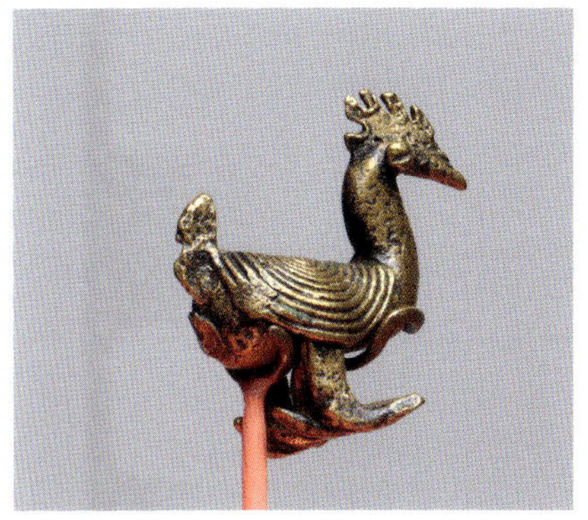

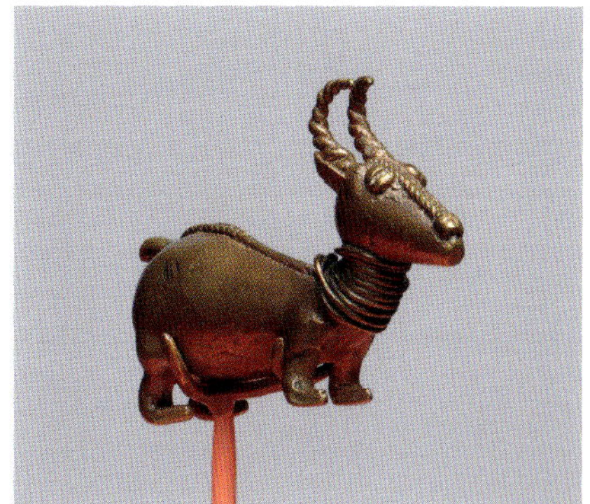

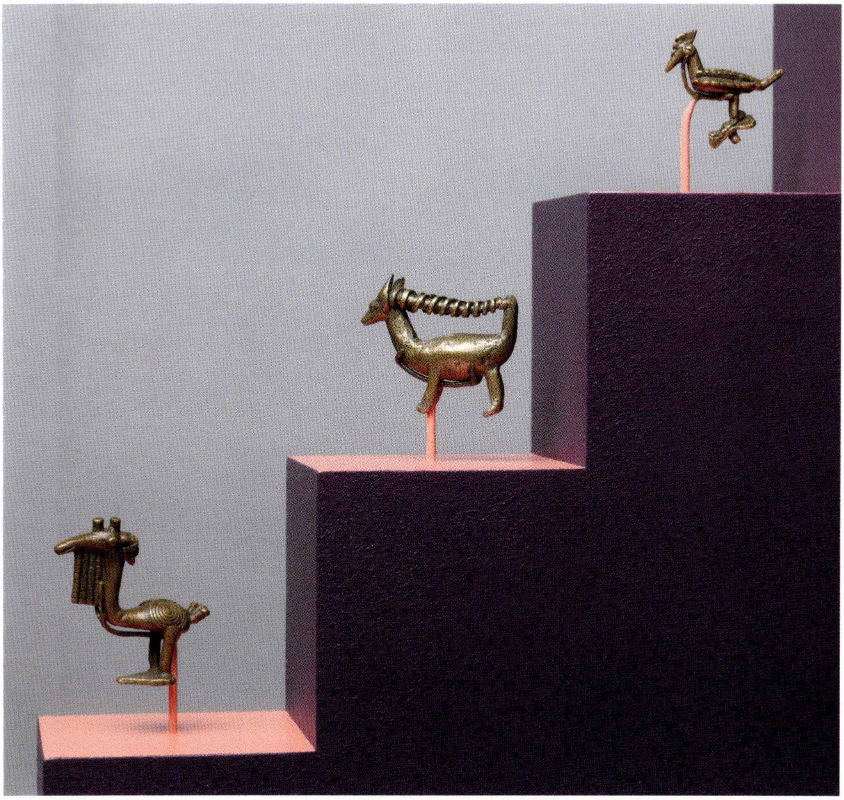

Top left: Baule artist, Bird-Shaped Gold Weight, early 1900s. Bronze, 1¼ × ⅝ × 1⅜ in. Anonymous gift, 2001.959.

Top right: Baule artist, Antelope-Shaped Gold Weight, early 1900s. Bronze, 1¼ × ½ × 1¾ in. Anonymous gift, 2001.958.

Above left to right: Baule artist, Bird-Shaped Gold Weight, early 1900s. Bronze, 1⅞ × ⅝ × 2 in. Anonymous gift, 2001.954. Baule artist, Antelope-Shaped Gold Weight, early 1900s. Bronze, 1⅜ × ⅜ × 1⅞ in. Anonymous gift, 2001.953. Ashanti artist, Bird-Shaped Gold Weight, early 1900s. Brass, 1⅜ × 1¼ × ½ in. Native Arts acquisition funds, 1948.601.

complexities of life, preeminent in West African folklore. Adinkra symbols were also featured as prints on cloth worn to important ceremonies (cat. 5).

Over time, the geometric patterns on the gold weights became more complex and figurative, with spirals, waves, and stylized representations of human figures and animals. These weights represented everyday objects, like shoes, tools, knives, and rope, as well as living beings like animals and people. Some figurines represented Akan proverbs.[11] The ability of an Akan speaker to communicate metaphorically was evidence of the speaker's wisdom and was fundamental to earning the respect of society as an elder.[12] The relationship between Akan proverbs and gold weight forms may indicate that they served as educational tools and mnemonic devices, helping children become fluent in their proverbial language.

In 1889, the Demonetization of Gold Dust Ordinance was passed in the Gold Coast, forbidding the use of gold dust and nuggets as currency. In 1896, the Weights and Measures Ordinance made it illegal to use gold weights.[13] Consequently, by the 1920s, the production of gold weights had declined, although the skill continues to this day through the work of some remarkable contemporary artists. Throughout the early and mid-twentieth century, European and American expatriates in Ghana and Côte d'Ivoire collected these objects, finding them easily at the markets and through personal contacts with owners. Our collection holds twenty-nine gold weights, as well as a scale, scoop, and measure. Nineteen of the weights were collected before the 1960s, when most African nations were gaining independence from colonial rule. The rest were collected between 1971 and 2001.

Commerce and Exchange on the East African Coast

In contrast to African trade on the western Atlantic coast, that of the eastern Indian Ocean coast was shaped by a long history of encounter not only with the West but also with the Arab world and present-day India. East Africans regularly traveled and migrated—both as free and enslaved people—since the first century. A first-century Greek merchant's guide, the *Periplus of the Erythraean Sea*, describes sailing voyages on the Red Sea and the East African coast.[14] In the account, the author describes the wealth of ivory, rhino horn, tortoise shell, and palm oil available in various East African city-states. This region, known

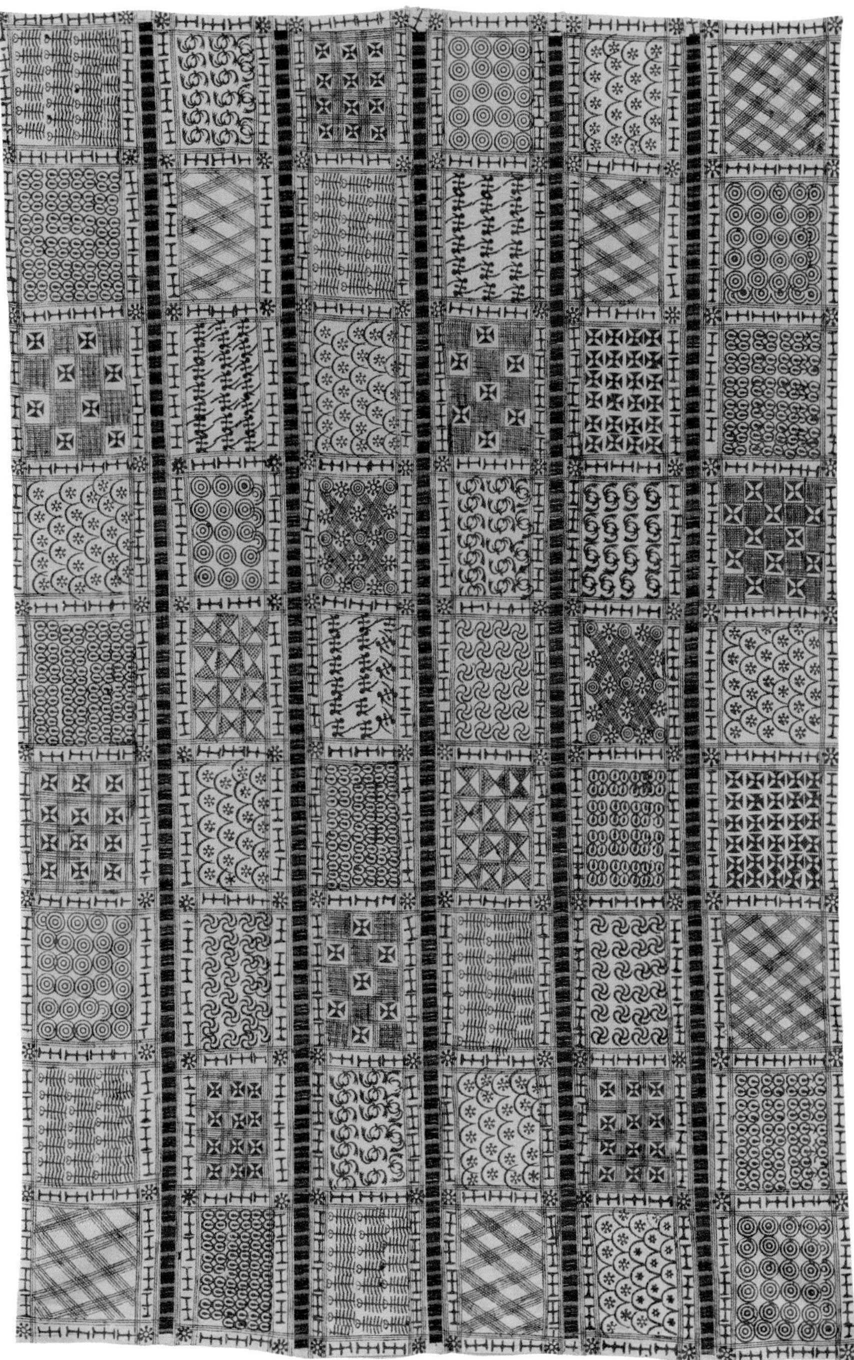

Cat. 5. Ashanti artist. Adinkra Cloth, before 1965. Silk, cotton, and dye, 135 × 88 in.
Gift of Mr. and Mrs. Peter Cook, 1975.171.

as the Swahili Coast, stretches from present-day Somalia in the north to Mozambique in the south. The word Swahili is derived from sawāhilī, a plural adjectival form of the Arabic word (يلِحَاوَس) meaning "of the coasts." The Swahili Coast is a contact zone of African, Arab, and other Indian Ocean cultures, where the shared practice of Islam also created and continues to foster a sense of unity among the different communities.

A Swahili hat (*kofia*), for instance, historically indicated Muslim affiliation, regardless of one's origin, all along the coast (cat. 6). In the nineteenth and twentieth centuries, with the onset of colonialism, the designs in different regions transformed, creating a space for Muslims to assert their refusal against European colonialism. In Zanzibar, the Swahili hat became a marker of higher social status among men who were not colonized. Today, in Tanzania, Swahili hats are worn as a form of national dress, even by men who don't affiliate with Islam.[15] Significantly, Africans living along the Indian Ocean had a very different understanding of what it means to be from Africa than their counterparts on the western coast, where identity was heavily influenced by the transatlantic slave trade and Western categories of race. On the eastern coast, cultural identities were not fixed in stone, leading these communities to translate and celebrate differences in commercial, social, and artistic ways.[16]

The network of trade covering the Indian Ocean and the Arab world ensured the distribution not only of materials but of artisans and designs.[17] In essence, local tastes could intermingle with external designs and materials to produce differing styles. Ornate chests, sometimes called Kuwaiti, Omani, or Zanzibari chests, were originally carved from tropical woods like teak or camphor in Gujarat, India, and shipped across the Indian Ocean by Arab and Indian traders (cat. 7).[18] More than mundane storage boxes, they held dowries, jewelry, and trade goods. Although they originated in India, artisans in Zanzibar, Kuwait, and Oman learned to make them with unique regional decorative features. As such, the chests made and sold in Zanzibar had unique designs that differentiated them from those sold in Kuwait or Oman. Indian Ocean epistemologies of identity and place, as expressed through the art and textiles of the time, challenge established notions about cultural difference and the movement of Africans across continents before colonization.[19]

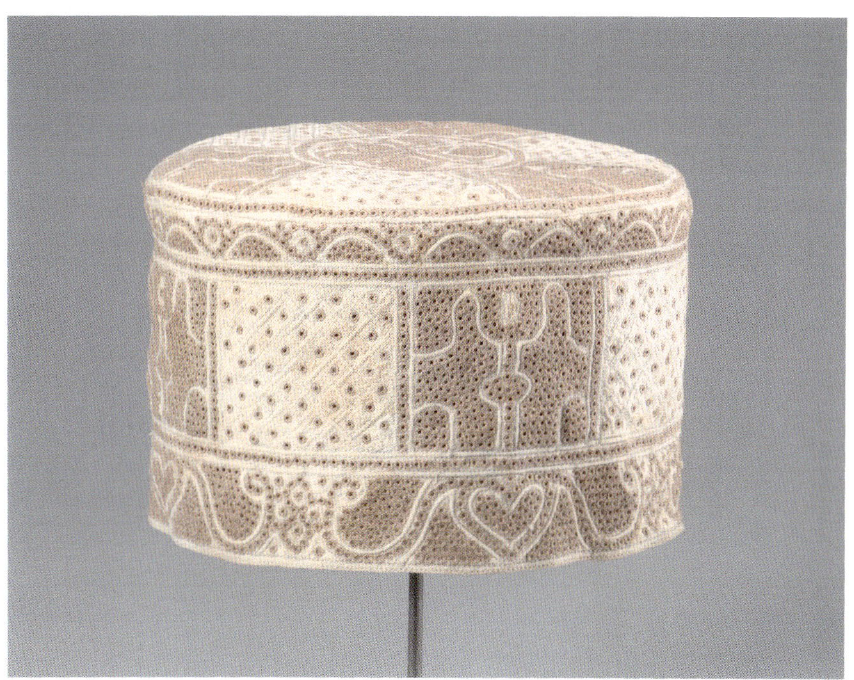

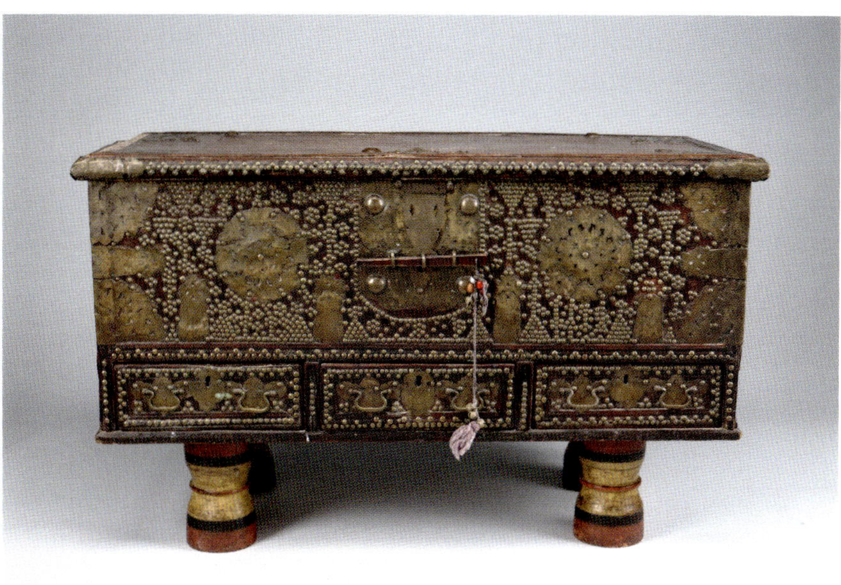

Top: Cat. 6. Swahili artist. Hat, c. 1960. Cotton and thread, 4½ × 6¾ in. dia.
Collection of Thelma R. Newman at the Denver Art Museum, Gift of Jay and Lee Newman, 1987.480.

Bottom: Cat. 7. Indian artist. Kuwaiti, Omani, or Zanzibari Wedding Chest, late 1800s. Wood with brass, other metals, and paint, 18½ × 44½ × 19⅝ in. Bequest of Carl Patterson, 2020.241A-I.

Kingship and Stools

For most African cultures, the symbol of authority for a chief or king was the stool. Some kingdoms and chiefdoms, especially those in central and West Africa, had and still have traditions of using stools in place of chairs and thrones. Stools from the grassland region of southwest Bamun (now Cameroon) were typically made for a community's ruler, who would assert his power by using it in ceremonies (cat. 8). The Bamun stool in the museum's collection is adorned with carved standing figures, who hold their arms upright, literally supporting the seat of their ruler[20]

The stool was also a symbol of the king's authority among the Akan. Similar to Indian Ocean artisans, who incorporated external designs into local tastes, as Akan artists encountered imported European wooden chairs with leather seats and backs, they incorporated some of those forms into their own designs for their rulers. The chair in our collection features a wooden frame adorned with antelope skin and brass tacks, suggesting that a minor ruler in the Akan community owned it (cat. 9).[21]

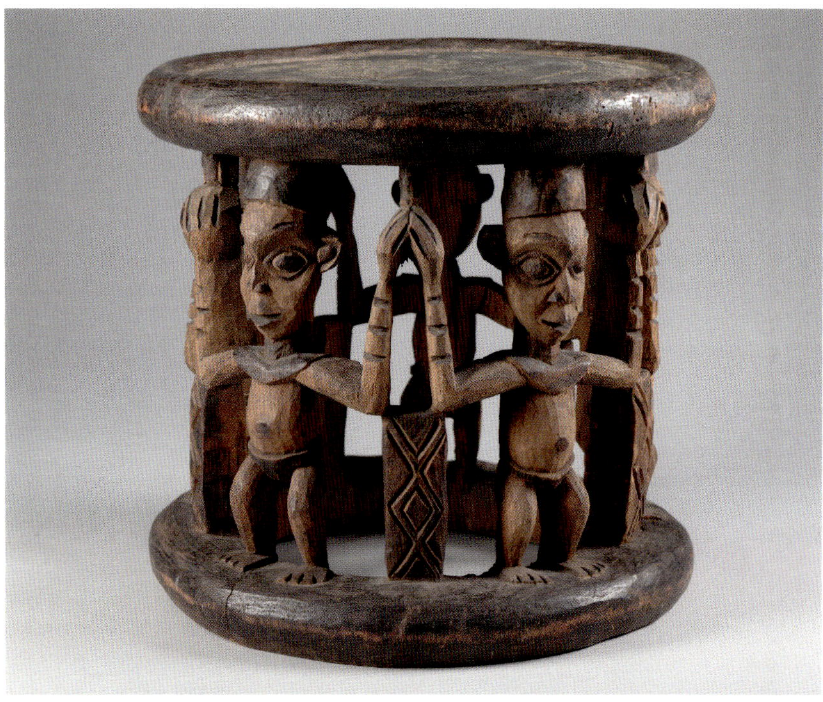

Cat. 8. Bamun artist. Stool, before 1953. Wood, 14¼ × 13⅝ × 13 in. Museum exchange with British Museum, London, 1953.903.

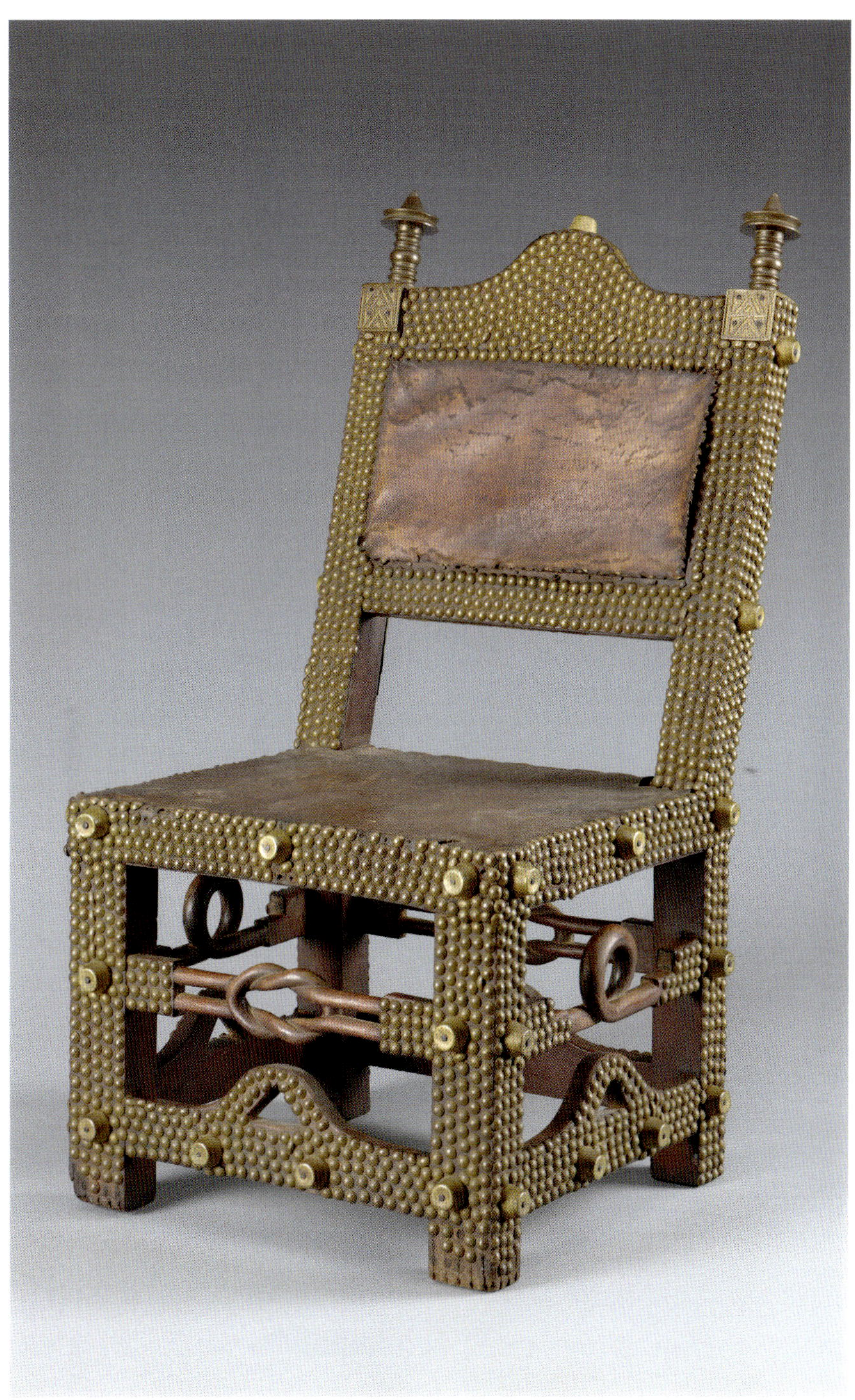

Cat. 9. Akan artist. Chair, c. 1950. Wood, brass, and antelope hide, 30½ × 17 × 15 in.
Gift of Mr. and Mrs. Robert Donner Jr., 1988.32.

African Spirituality and Masks

Spirituality is integral to every African culture. People connect with the worlds of the gods, spirits, and ancestors through prayers, invocations, incantations, and dance. These are performed in public or private settings and are often accompanied by food, drink, and, occasionally, animal sacrifices. Masks are frequently used in such ceremonies, serving as a connecting point between the spiritual and physical worlds and acting as more than mere visual art. Given the diversity of Africa and the different cultural and spiritual contexts, the specific meaning and interpretation of masks is contextual. But their core purpose remains to deeply connect communities through storytelling, religious practice, and maintenance of social structures.[23]

Masks are made by men and, in almost all African societies, are worn only by men. One of the few exceptions is the Mende community in present-day Sierra Leone and Liberia, where the all-woman Sowei secret society wears them. Some masks are used in masquerades during initiation rites to symbolize the transition from childhood to adulthood, others are worn during hunting rituals, and others are used to invoke protection from evil spirits or to usher departed loved ones into the afterlife. They offer illusion, ambivalence, and paradox, giving a visual representation of abstract concepts central to African cosmologies.

Masks and masquerades are both more and less than what they appear to be. They can be comic and lighthearted or deeply serious. They are consistent in their creativity and imagination, blending art and artifice. Masquerade dress components are many and varied, but they all begin with the active human body as the model. In their most imaginative extensions into the otherworldly, they appear to depart the human realm entirely to enter fantasy or pure invention. And even if the masked character mirrors a human being, it embodies transformation as a defining characteristic; the wearer is himself, and simultaneously, he is more than himself. During a masquerade, the masker will wear clothing different from what he wears on a daily basis, allowing him to keep his identity secret. Because his face is never seen, he can exist as a member of society while also retaining the secret identity of a masker.[24]

Yoruba Sacred Art

The Yoruba are renowned for their prolific artistry and craftsmanship. Most of the historical Yoruba artworks in the museum's collection date from between the end of the nineteenth century and the mid-twentieth century, an exciting period in Yoruba history when older art forms were finding new, contemporary expressions. Yoruba cosmology understands the universe as structured across two interpenetrating realms: ayé, the visible world of the living and òrun, the invisible world of the divine, the departed ancestors and the unborn. These realms, although different, are not separate from each other—the physical, visible world is a manifestation of the invisible, and every living being carries within them an unborn spirit partner (Enikeji).[25]

This dualistic universe is governed by Olódùmarè (or Olórun), regarded as too pure to be approached or worshipped directly by human beings. Mediating between Olódùmarè and living beings are the Orishas. They are divine intermediaries whose purpose is to govern specific domains of the natural and human world. Living beings are divided into two categories: the Ègún, who are deceased ancestors, and humans who are living in the visible world. The Ègún remain present in the lives of their descendants through divination, prayers, and offerings.[26]

Within this cosmology, everything in the universe exists in a dynamic tension between two principles, Ire, the forces of good fortune, and Ibi, the forces of disruption and misfortune. Through Ibi, the spiritual forces associated with death, disease, and affliction operate in the world.[27] These forces are known as Ajogun and are not evil in the theological sense. Instead, they are necessary disruptors who act as counterweights within a cosmological reality that needs both order and interference to remain in balance.[28] Consequently, Yoruba sacred art does not depict a struggle between opposing forces. Rather, it gives material form to the ongoing negotiation between Ire and Ibi.

Ifá divination embodies this active relationship between the principles of Ire and Ibi. Ifá is the body of knowledge and religious system through which the Yoruba understand and negotiate the forces of ayé (visible) and òrun (invisible) in everyday life.[29] The Orishas mediate between Olódùmarè and living beings to make this possible. Òrúnmìlà, the Orisha of wisdom, knowledge, and fate, reveals the will of Olódùmarè through the sacred texts of the Odù Ifá—256 sacred signs each containing hundreds of verses, proverbs, and prescriptions, all of which cover the breadth of life's situations. Ifá, in this way, is more than a religion: It is also a philosophical system that dictates everyday life in Yoruba culture.[30]

Èṣù is the Orisha of the crossroads who mediates between the human and divine realms. All sacrifices and offerings made to the Orishas first pass through Èṣù. Also known as Elegba or Legba, Èṣù is one of the most recognizable Orishas in the Yoruba pantheon. A complex god with many facets and roles, he is best known as the trickster god and the god of chance, unpredictability, and accidents.[31] He is a god of dualities and contradictions; while he thrives on disorder and confusion, he is also a servant and companion of Òrúnmìlà. He is often portrayed as having two faces, one on the front and the other on his back, representing trickery, opportunity, and watchfulness (cat. 13). Although generally referred to as "he," Èṣù has both masculine and feminine qualities that are often expressed in dual faces. Èṣù requires constant appeasement, and the cowrie shells on the Denver Art Museum's example are meant to serve as payment to convince him to deliver messages rather than play tricks.[32]

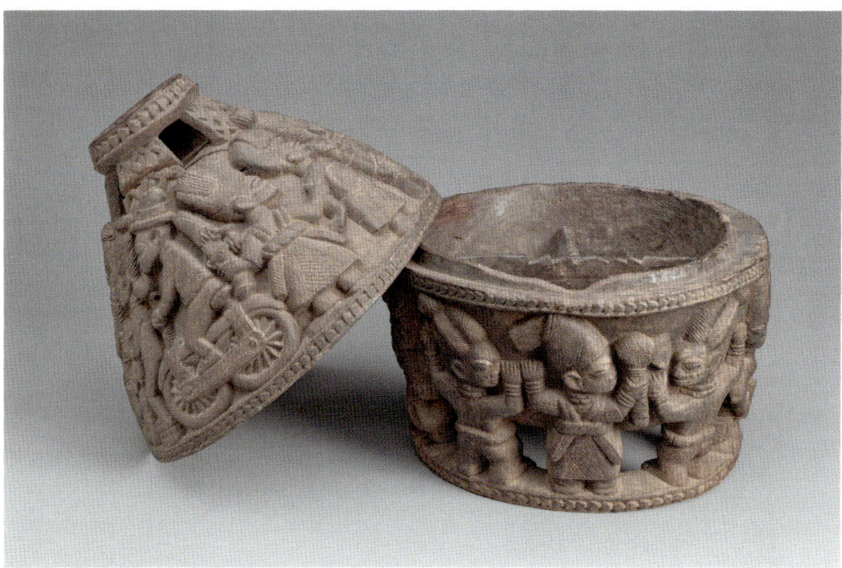

Cat. 12. Areogun of Osi-Ilorin (Yoruba, 1875-1954). Ifá Divination Bowl, early 1900s. Iroko wood, 23¼ high and 17⅜ in. dia. Gift of Mary and Robert Cumming, 2025.649A-B.

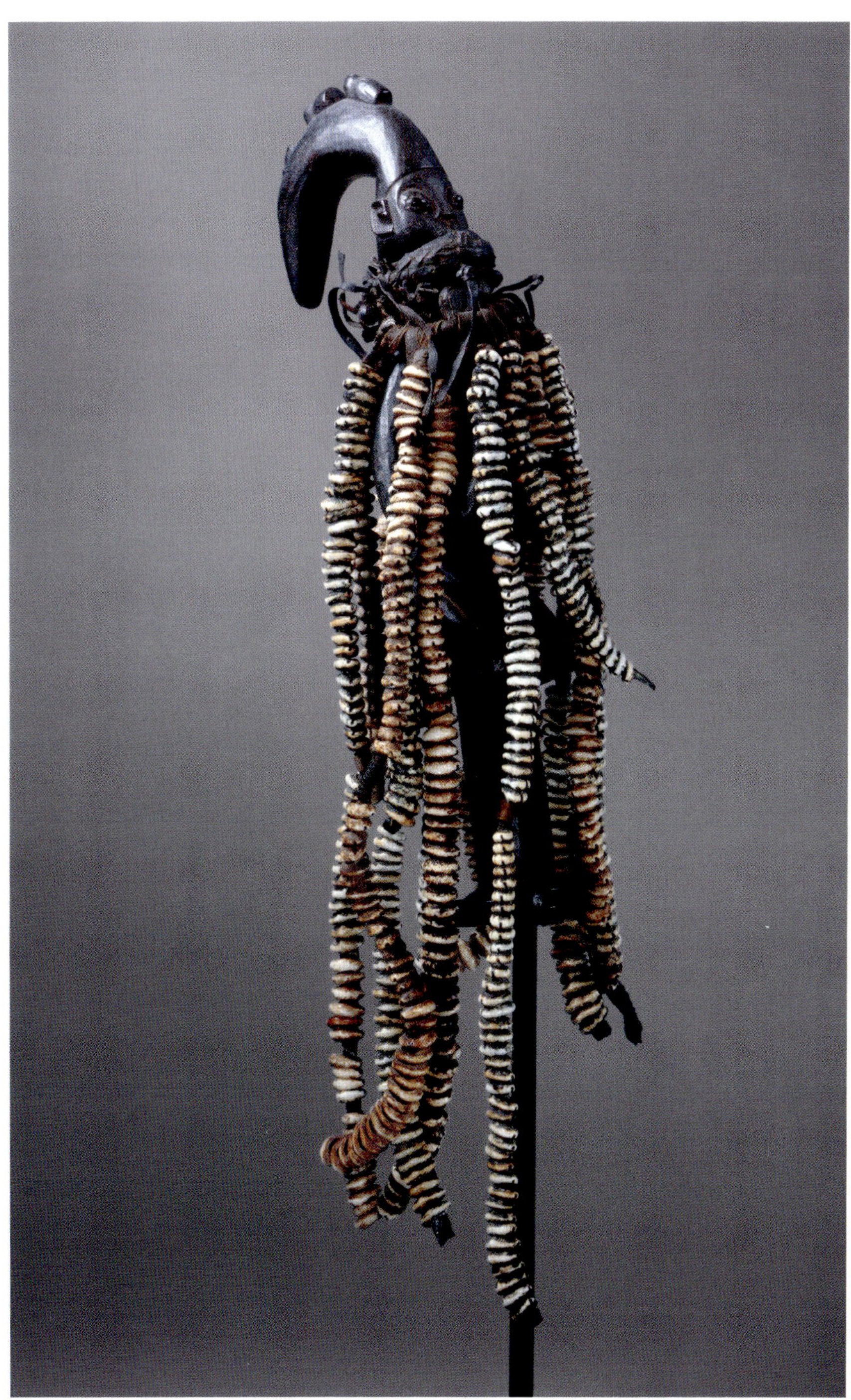

Cat. 13. Yoruba artist. Èṣù Elegba Figure, 1900s. Wood, leather, and cowrie shells, 31 × 24 × 7 in. Gift of Maureen and Dan Nidess, 1985.296.

The living being who navigates Ifá on behalf of others is the Babaláwo. Meaning "father of secrets," he is an initiated diviner who has memorized the 256 sacred signs of the Odù Ifá. He seeks the will of Òrúnmìlà through a divination tray (Opon Ifá) on which he throws sixteen sacred palm nuts and then interprets their positions.[33] When not in use, the nuts are stored in a carved wooden divination bowl (Agere Ifá) (cat. 12). The carved figure supporting the bowl is a woman kneeling in a posture of supplication and reverence, speaking to the significant place of women in Ifá and Yoruba culture at large.

Alongside the Babaláwo and complementary to his spiritual practice is the Onísègùn, a herbalist and healer. This person can be male or female, and their practice is not through divination but through direct engagement with the material world.[34] The Onísègùn uses a metal staff to honor Òsányìn, the Orisha of healing who brings completeness and well-being (cat. 14). The staff is made of iron and also refers to another Orisha, Ògún, who makes the herbal healer's work possible through metal tools. In the example from the museum's collection, the central bird hovers over smaller, abstract birds, symbolizing the power to control or eliminate forces of misfortune to heal.[35]

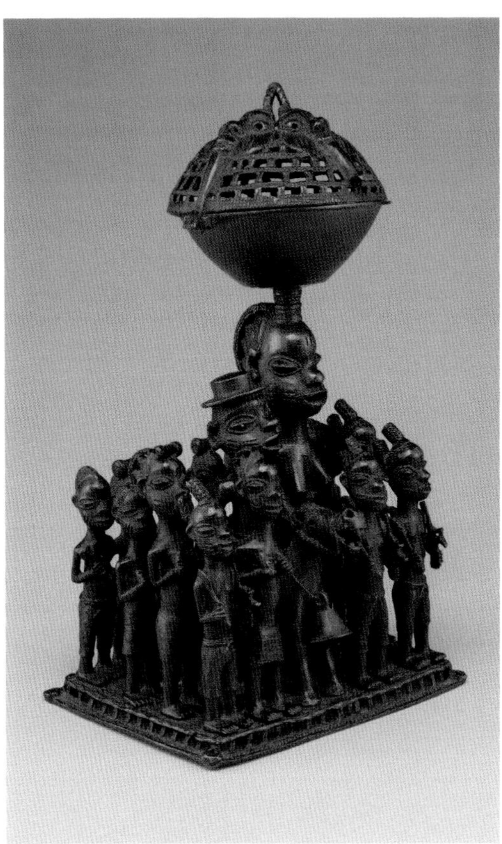

Yoruba artist. Incense Burner Depicting a Bride and Groom Carrying a Baby, before 1952. Brass, 12⅜ × 7⅛ × 5¾ in. Native Arts acquisition funds, 1954.556.

At the third tier of the Yoruba divine hierarchy are the Ègún, the deceased ancestors who serve as spiritual guides and continue to influence the lives of

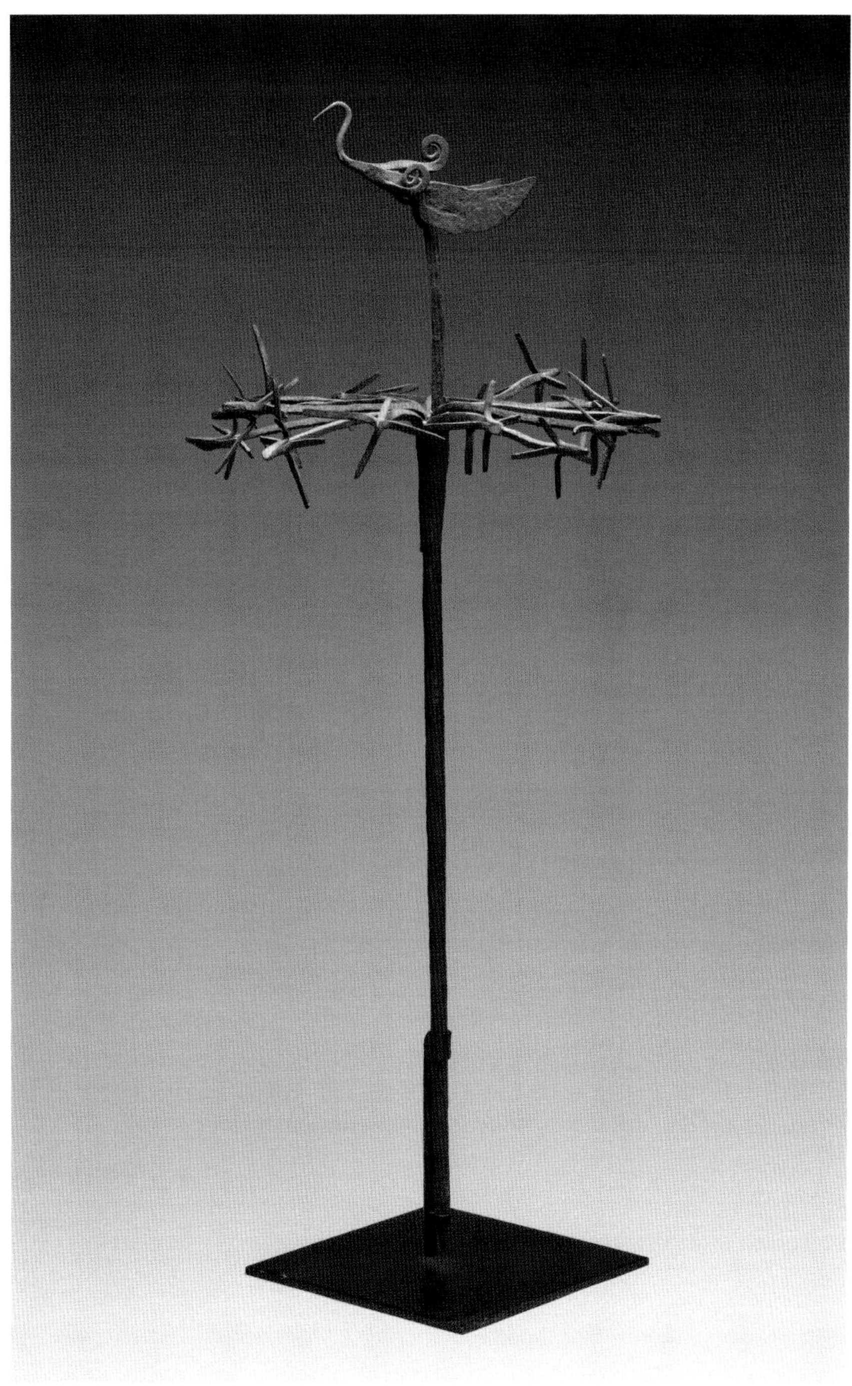

Cat. 14. Yoruba artist. Òsányìn Staff, 1900s. Wrought iron, 23⅞ × 11 in. Gift of Mary and Robert Cumming, 2015.670.

their living descendants. They are consulted alongside the Orishas through divination, prayers, and offerings.[36] Their presence in the community is made visible through the Egungun masquerade, when the ancestors visit the living to offer guidance, settle disputes, and affirm the connection between the dead and the living.[37]

The cosmological system described above did not remain contained within Yoruba culture in Africa. Between the early sixteenth century and the late nineteenth century, the violent transatlantic slave trade carried Ifá across the Atlantic.[38] Ifá became the root from which several distinct religious traditions grew in the diaspora: Santería and Lucumí in Cuba, Candomblé and Umbanda in Brazil, and Trinidad Orisha in the Caribbean.[39] Enslaved peoples merged Ifá's structures with Catholic iconography, creating new religious practices that have since become independent traditions with their own liturgies. Yoruba sacred art represents a living system that has survived dispossession, suppression, and transformation. The artworks described here are part of that: local in their making and global in their reach.[40]

Yoruba Secret Societies: Masks and Masquerades

Secret societies in Yoruba culture exist to intervene in the community's problems. They act as intermediaries between the living and the dead. Some of the most important ones are the Gelede, Epa, and Egungun. The Gelede secret society pays homage to the power of elderly women and is primarily found among the Ketu, Yewa, Ohori, Anago, and Awori subgroups of the Yoruba. Older Yoruba women are believed to have direct links with deities and can harness that power for good or bad. During Gelede festivals, men wear helmet masks carved in the form of a human face (cat. 15). On top of the carved head, there is either an elaborate coiffure or a carved representation of human activity.[41] Every year, Yoruba men wear Gelede masks during masquerades to celebrate feminine power and ensure the community's well-being. They seek the help of elderly women to prevent disease, induce rain, increase fertility, benefit from supernatural forces during wartime, and honor the dead. The elderly women are affectionately called *awon iya wa* (our mothers) and receive special homage at the beginning of a Gelede masquerade to encourage them to allow the community to benefit from their extraordinary powers, especially procreation.[42]

The Epa secret society (also known as Elefon) makes masks that vary significantly according to the town where they appear. Their masks typically depict nobles, ancestral spirits, deities, and cultural heroes. They can weigh as much as fifty pounds or more and are worn during funerals, agricultural cycles, and rites of passage. Characteristically, they are composed of many elements, usually a human-face helmet topped by an elaborate standing figure (cat.16). When not in use, these masks are kept in shrines, where they are honored with libations and prayers.[43] The helmet portion of the mask in the museum's collection is double-sided, or Janus-faced. A prominent female figure and her twins tower over the top of the helmet. In Yoruba culture, twins are believed to possess supernatural powers. In ancient times, the Yoruba used to reject and sometimes sacrifice twins, but today, their birth is an occasion of great rejoicing.[44]

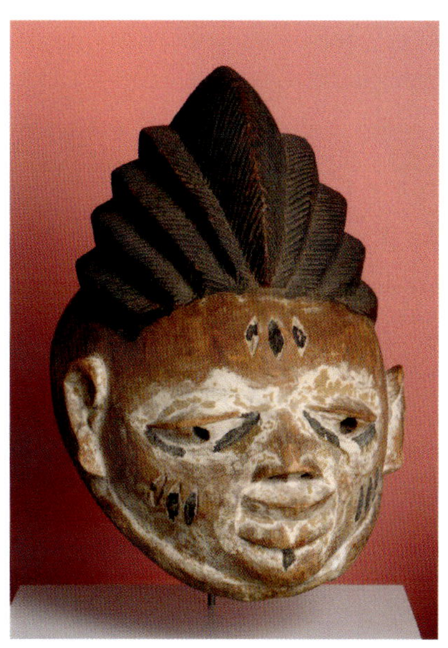

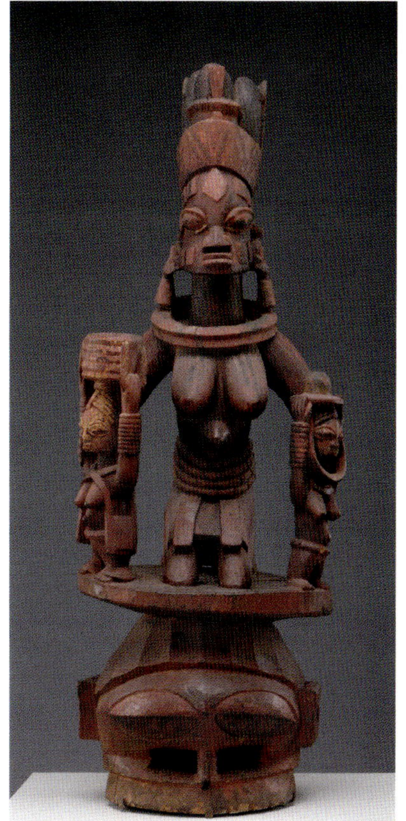

Top right: Cat. 15. Yoruba artist. Gelede Mask, before 1953. Wood and pigment, 8¼ × 8¼ × 13 in. Museum exchange with British Museum, London, 1953.898.

Right: Cat. 16. Osamuko (Yoruba, active early 1900s). Epa Helmet Mask with Iyabeji (Mother of Twins), c. 1900. Painted wood, 46 × 15 × 16 in. Native Arts acquisition funds, 1970.802.

It is believed that they can bestow happiness, health, and prosperity on their family—though they could equally bring disaster, disease, and death. When they are born, they are treated with respect, love, and care so they can reciprocate the same to their family.[45]

The Egungun secret society exists to connect ancestral spirits to their living descendants. Egungun masks are worn in annual masquerades by men who represent deceased ancestors capable of bringing good fortune or punishing the guilty (cat. 17). They also appear during festivities following the death of a dignitary or during initiation ceremonies. They exhibit considerable stylistic variation, with the principal defining characteristic being the loose, body-covering costume rather than the standard headdress. During the masquerade, the multiple layers of cloth hanging beneath the headpiece conceal the wearer.[46] For Yoruba people, the dance celebrates the connection between ancestral spirits and their living descendants.

Beyond masks, Yoruba sculptors also carved artworks to decorate palace and shrine doors, as well as the posts supporting roofs and verandas (cat. 18, p. 34). Among the most famous of these artists was Olowe of Ise (c. 1873–1938), who carved posts in a recognizable angular style for the palace located in southern Ekiti, Nigeria. The elongated and dynamic characteristics of his work are shown in the complex veranda post in the museum's collection. The theme of the equestrian figure, prevalent in Yoruba palatial art, reflects the status attached to owning horses.[47]

Northern Nigeria: Igboland

In northern Nigeria, in Igboland, men wear the Agbobho Mmwo masks, which translates into "maiden spirits." The mask is worn during the Fame of Maidens celebration, which honors important deities and ancestors (cat. 19, p. 35). The men who dance with Mmwo masks wear colorful, tight-fitting fiber costumes and entertain the watching crowd with exaggerated versions of women's dances. They use masquerade dances to teach young Igbo women ideals of physical beauty, morality, and social roles. The small, well-balanced features of the face, small tattoos, and the white pigment reflect Igbo ideals of beauty.[48]

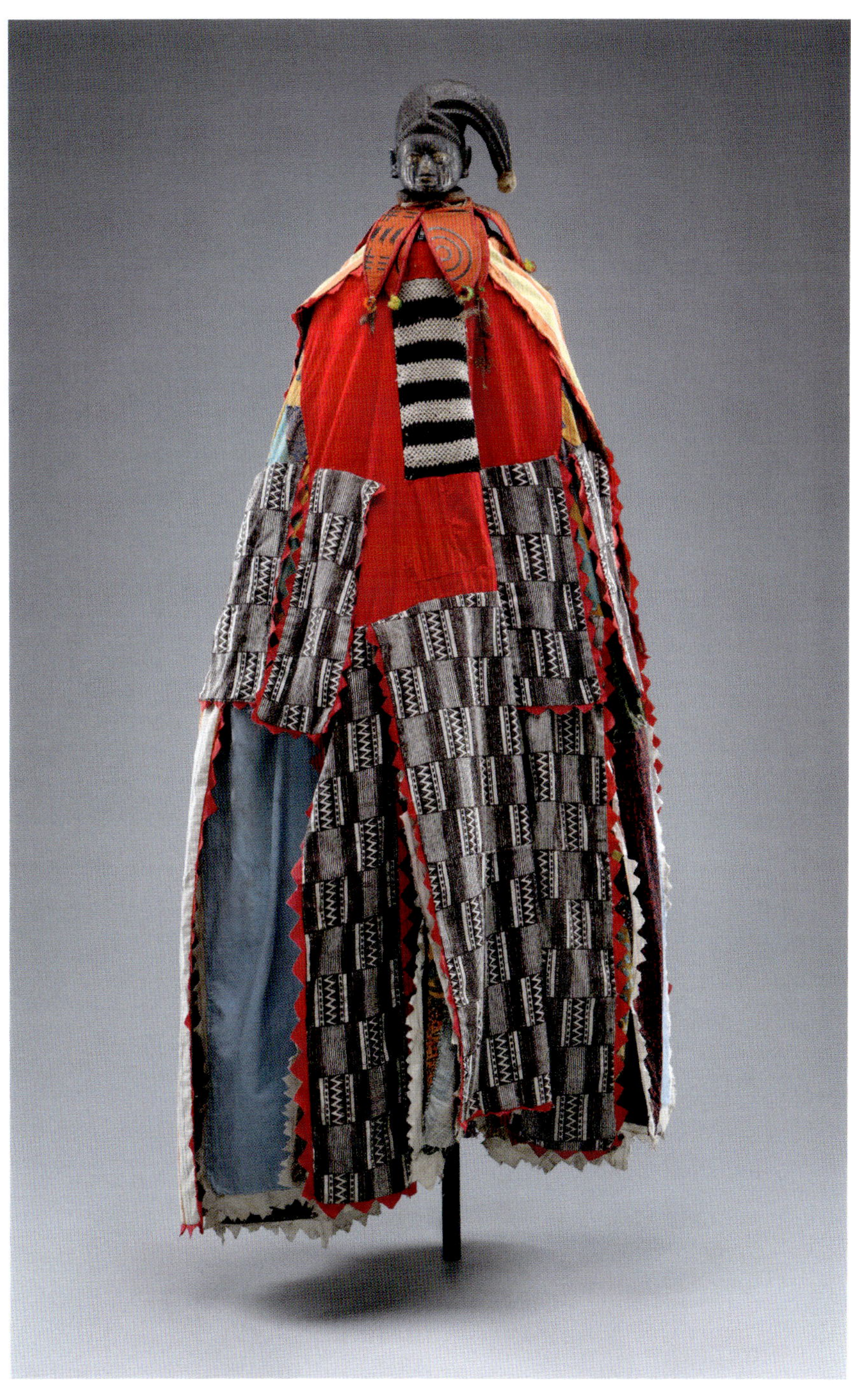

Cat. 17. Yoruba artist. Egungun Masquerade Outfit, late 1900s. Cotton and wood, 64 × 51½ × 10 in. Gift of Tim and Bobbi Hamill, 2009.347A-B.

Okoroshi masks are convex and oval, representing the Igbo water spirit, Owu (cat. 20). They have a hemispherical chin below a pursed mouth, with lips perforated at the center and inset with blocky teeth. Above their triangular nostrils are lozenge-shaped eyes, indented and perforated, set under high, arching brows. These masks are worn during the six-week rainy season, and more than forty distinct personas perform daily for over a month in the masquerade. Dancers wear male and female Okoroshi masks differentiated by color and facial features. The female masks represent good and beautiful spirits and are white-faced with delicate features. The male masks represent bad spirits and are blackened with distorted forms and animal features. This mask in the museum's collection is probably female because of its now-faded white color, delicate features, and coiffure.[49]

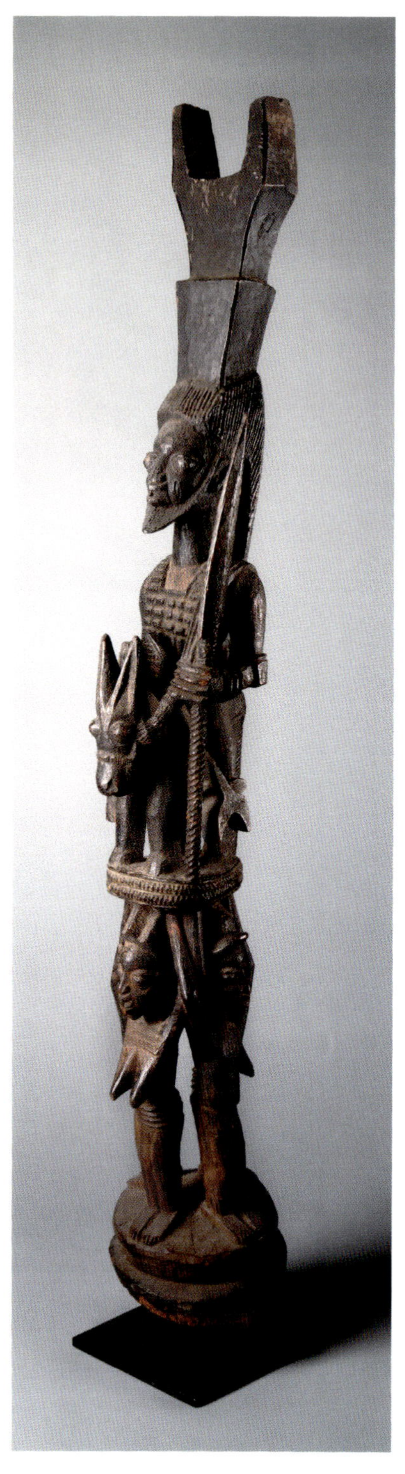

Cat. 18. Olowe of Ise (Yoruba, c. 1873–1938). House Post, late 1920s. Wood, 69 × 10 × 10 in. Funds from 1996 Collectors' Choice and partial gift of Valerie Franklin, 1996.260.

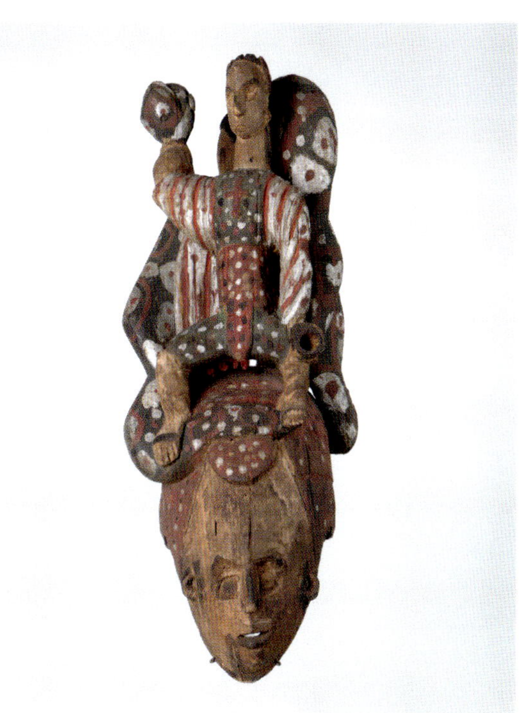

Cat. 19. Igbo artist. Mmwo Mask, 1920s. Painted wood, 5½ × 11 × 11 in. Gift of Paul Shaffer, 1977.78.

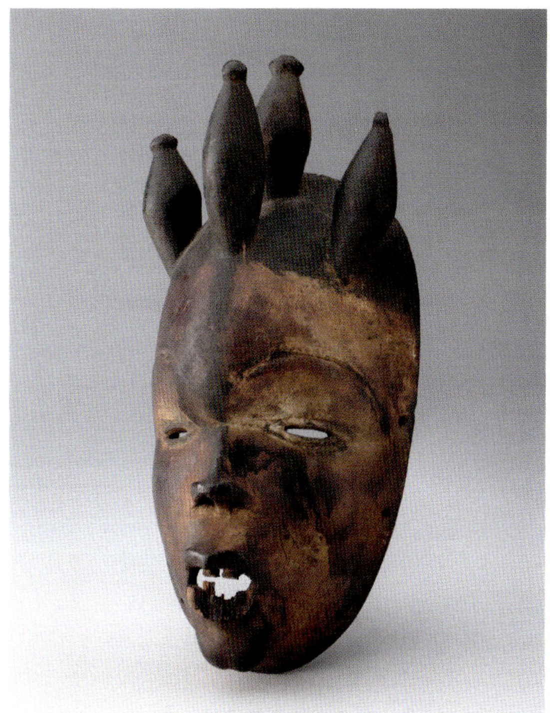

Cat. 20. Igbo artist. Okoroshi Mask, 1900s. Painted wood, 9½ × 4 in. Anonymous gift, 2001.1124.

Female Secret Societies: Mende Sowei Mask

In the Mende culture of present-day Sierra Leone and Liberia, the Sowei mask is one of the most prominent and recognizable. There are two distinct societies within the Mende—the all-male Poro and the all-female Sande. Both societies educate and train younger Mende men and women in preparation for their initiation into adulthood. Sowei helmet masks represent one of the few instances in which masks are used exclusively by and for African women (cat. 21). The museum's example is crafted from wood and features a monochromatic finish made from vegetable dye. The mask's features mirror ideals of Mende feminine beauty—petite and delicate neck, face, and coiffure. The Sande teaches women the necessary skills to prepare them for motherhood and the expectations of women. When the girls have completed their training, they participate in a coming-of-age ritual, signifying they have successfully achieved adulthood. At the ceremony, Sande officials wear the mask while dancing, embodying the spirit of the society. Because it is a helmet mask, it is worn over the head, with the rest of the dancer's body concealed by blackened raffia strands and fabric.[50]

Gabon Masks: Ngil Society and Punu Mask

The Fang community, in what is now Gabon, had a secret men-only society known as the Ngil, which means gorilla. The masks they wore, called Ngil masks, had arched eyebrows and a broad, rounded forehead meant to model a gorilla's face. (cat. 22, p. 38). They were made of wood and coated with kaolin clay, giving them their white color, which was associated with the spirits of ancestors, death, and male virility. Strips of raffia were attached to the mask. The Ngil were a powerful society that served as a force for social control through ritual and intimidation. Operating only at night, Ngil members wore the white masks to punish sorcerers and administer justice, maintaining the community's peace. Around 1910, the French colonial administration banned the Ngil society and outlawed its judicial activities. By the 1920s, they discontinued all Ngil rites, significantly impacting the society's remaining influence and leading to the decline in the creation of its masks and objects.[51] This mask in the museum's collection is one of the best few remaining examples in existence today in the global North. Despite the discontinuation of the secret society, Ngil masks

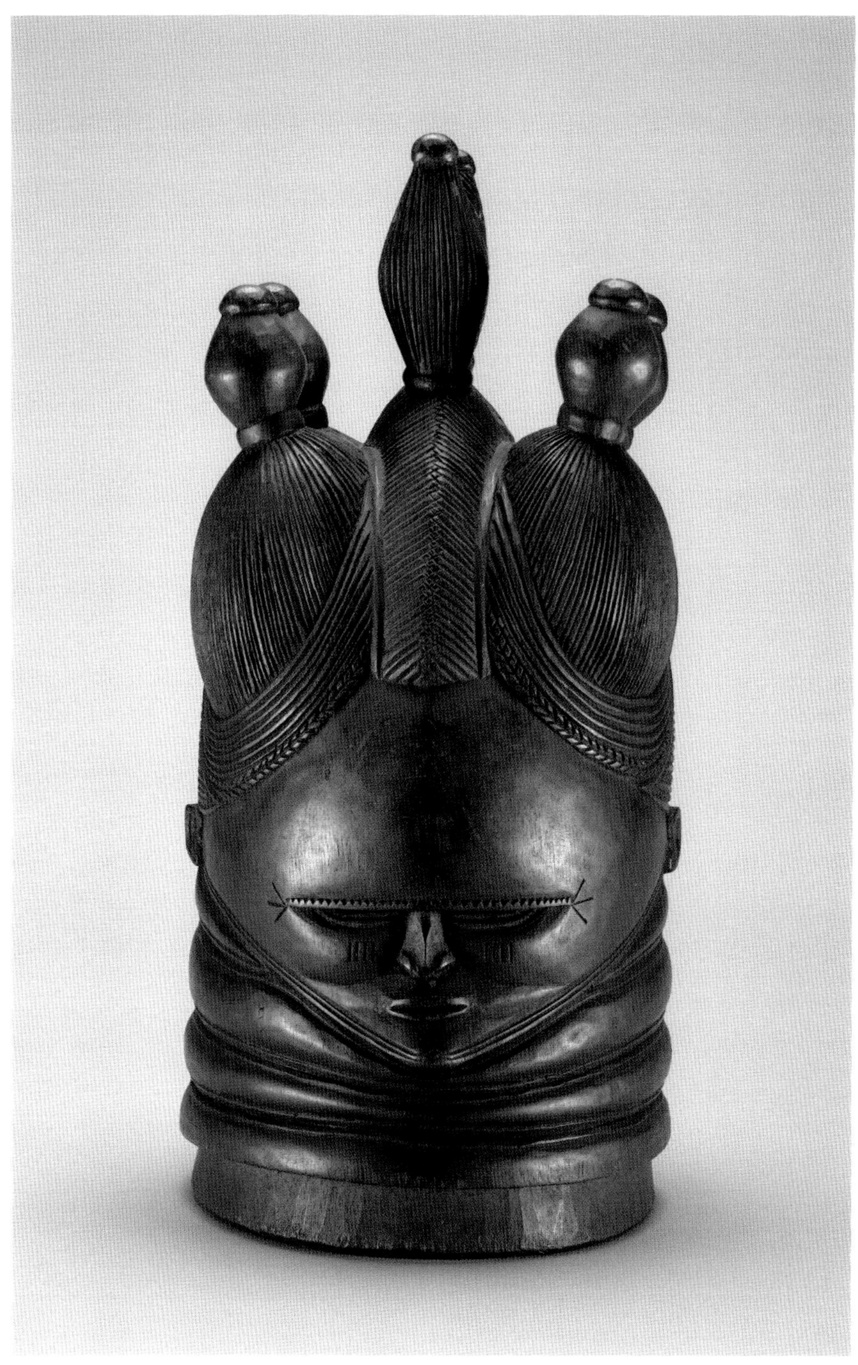

Cat. 21. Mende artist. Sowei Mask, late 1800s. Dyed wood, 17 × 7¾ × 8¾ in. Native Arts acquisition funds, 1949.4178.

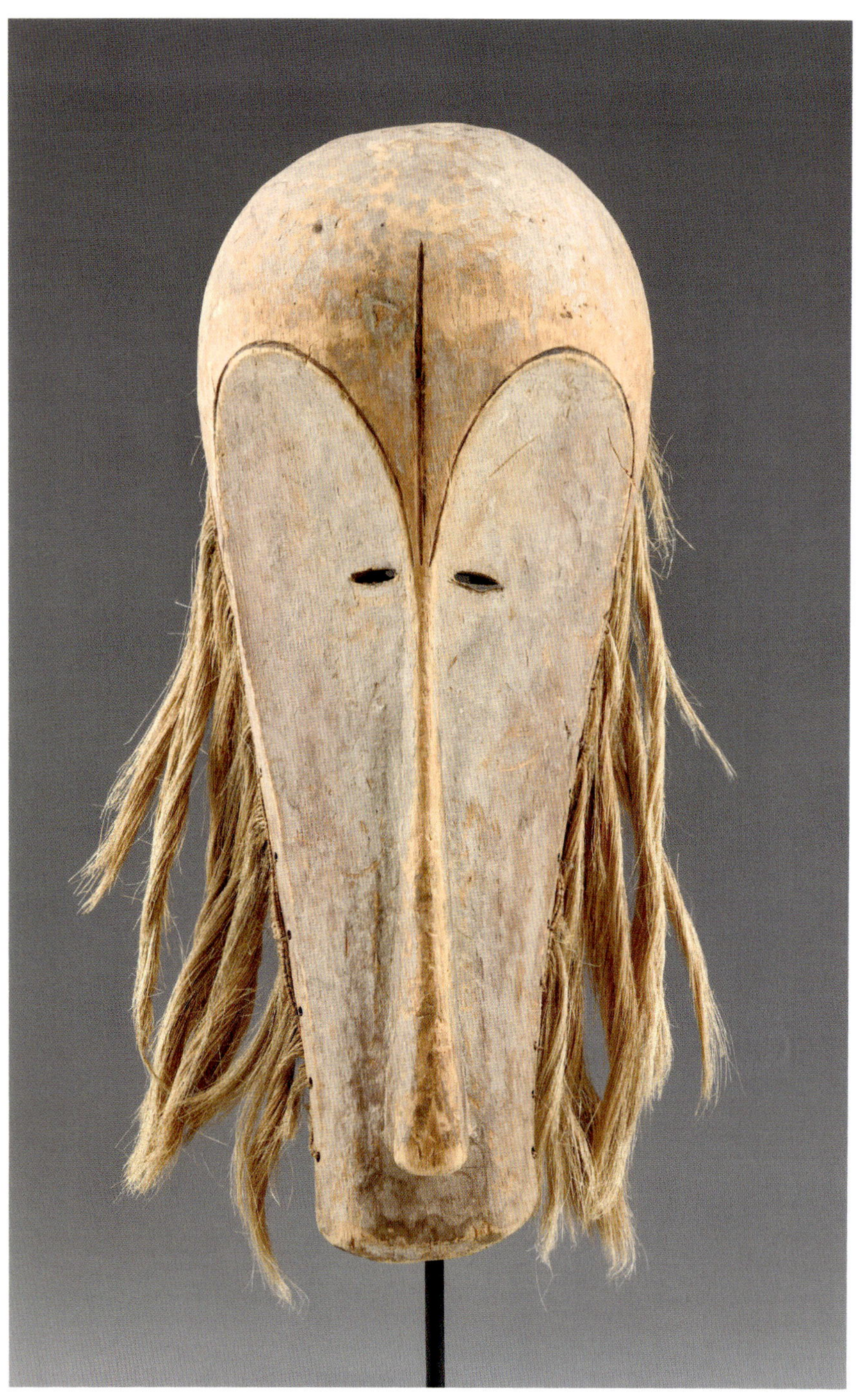

Cat. 22, Fang artist. Ngil Mask, late 1800s. Wood, fiber, and kaolin clay, 22 × 8¾ × 12½ in.
Gift of Fred H. Riebling, 1942.443.

played an important role in defining modern art and design outside of Africa. Their distinct aesthetic, spiritual, and cultural characteristics as well as emphasis on abstraction were welcomed by modern Western artists eager to move away from classical representation. Notable artists like Pablo Picasso, George Braque, and Amedeo Modigliani integrated African-inspired stylistic elements into their works. In particular, Picasso's *Les Demoiselles d'Avignon* (1906, Museum of Modern Art, New York) features a distorted mask-like face that reflects his inspiration from the Fang culture.[52]

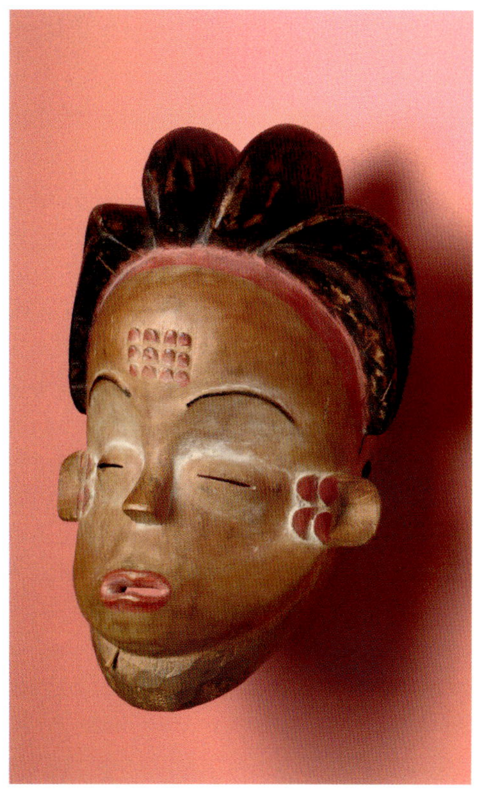

Cat. 23. Punu artist. Punu Mask, 1900s. Wood and pigment, 14 × 9 × 7 in. Funds from the Collectors' Choice Benefit, 1985, 1985.6.

The Punu mask was introduced to Western collectors in the early twentieth century (cat. 23). They were an enigma to art historians, who believed that the unique features were influenced by Asian aesthetics rather than those of Gabon (they were also prevalent in the Democratic Republic of the Congo). Punu masks were worn by virtuosic male performers of the *mukudj* (stilt dance), who towered impressively over viewers while making complex dance moves and astonishing feats of acrobatics. The artists of these masks would do his best to capture the likeness of the woman he considered most beautiful in his community. Kaolin clay was applied to the surface of the mask, allowing the artist to celebrate the beauty of a mortal woman while also transforming her into a transcendent being.[53]

Ivory Coast Masks: Mblo (Yaure Mask) and Kpnyungo

The Senufo are a West African group comprising diverse subgroups that live in a large region spanning the present-day northern Côte d'Ivoire, southeastern Mali, western Burkina Faso, and northwestern Ghana. They are famous for their objects that feature their cultural themes and religious beliefs. Similar to the Mende, they also have an all-men secret society known as the Poro. Senufo mask carvers combine features of intimidating animals, including those of the buffalo, crocodile, warthog, and antelope, to create a hybrid form (cat. 24). This Kponyungo mask was worn with a deep-red one-piece suit at the funeral of a Poro member. During the funeral, masqueraders beat hand drums to honor the deceased, ward off evil spirits, and attest to the society's strength.[54]

For the Baule in present-day Côte d'Ivoire, the Mblo mask was brought out for entertainment at the Gbagba masquerade (cat. 25). To perform, a masker in a cloth costume would conceal his face with a small wooden mask and dance for the audience, accompanied by drummers, singers, other dancers, and orators, in a series of skits. The masquerade brought respite from everyday chores, allowing community members to socialize, mourn, feast, and even court.[55] The dance associated with this mask has not been practiced since the 1980s and has been replaced by newer masks and performance styles.

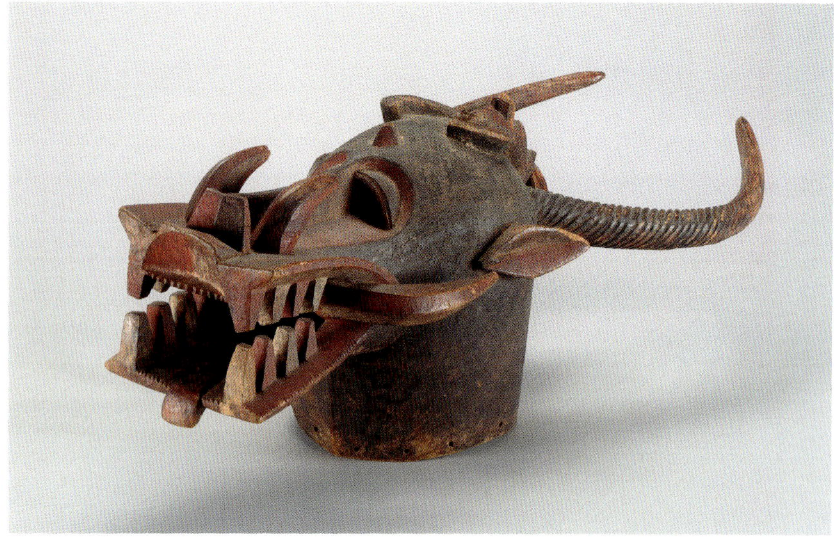

Cat. 24. Senufo artist. Kponyungo (Funeral Head) Mask, before 1957. Painted wood, 34½ × 14½ × 12 in. Museum exchange with Julius Carlebach, 1957.205.

Democratic Republic of the Congo: Kholuka Mask

Kholuka masks among the Yaka in the Democratic Republic of the Congo are used in the Nkanda traditional ceremony that marks the end of young men's initiation ritual, transitioning them to adulthood (cat. 26, p. 42). For one to three years, boys are separated from women and educated by male elders about their duties as adults in Yaka culture. Yaka masks represent the ancestors who oversee the fertility of young men and the celebration of their reintegration after a period of seclusion. They are won on the head or held briefly in front of the face.[56]

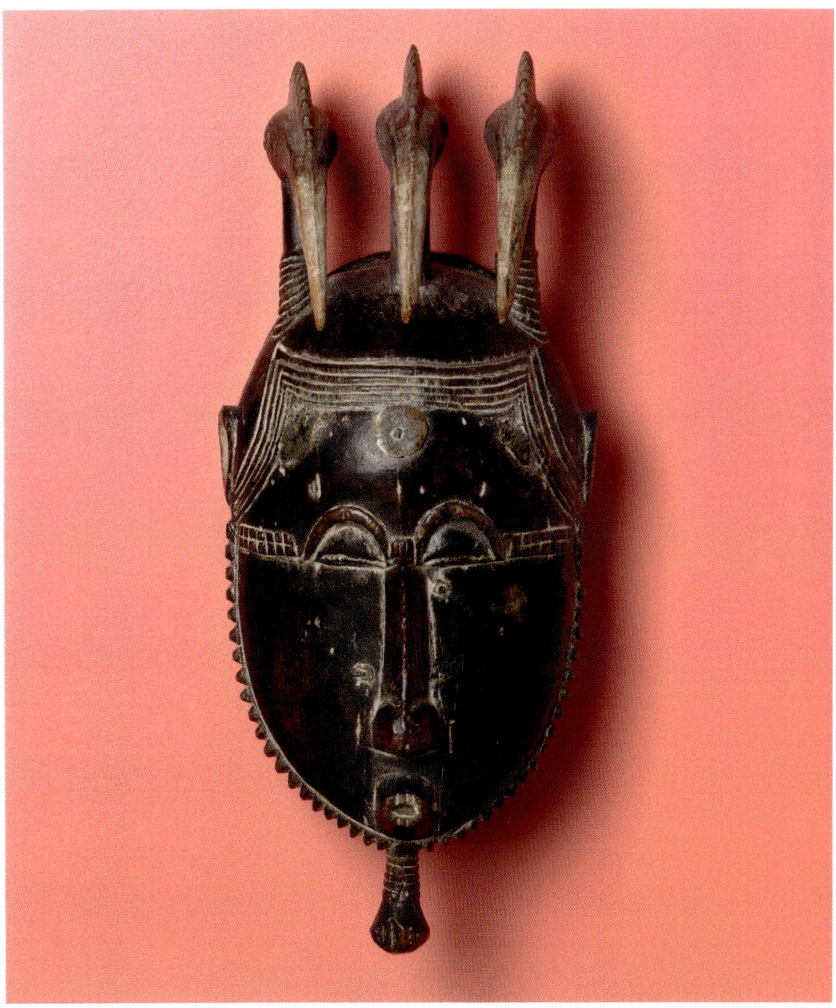

Cat. 25. Yaure artist. Mblo Mask, late 1800s–early 1900s. Carved wood with pigment and metal, 15 × 6½ × 4 in. Anonymous gift, 2001.1111.

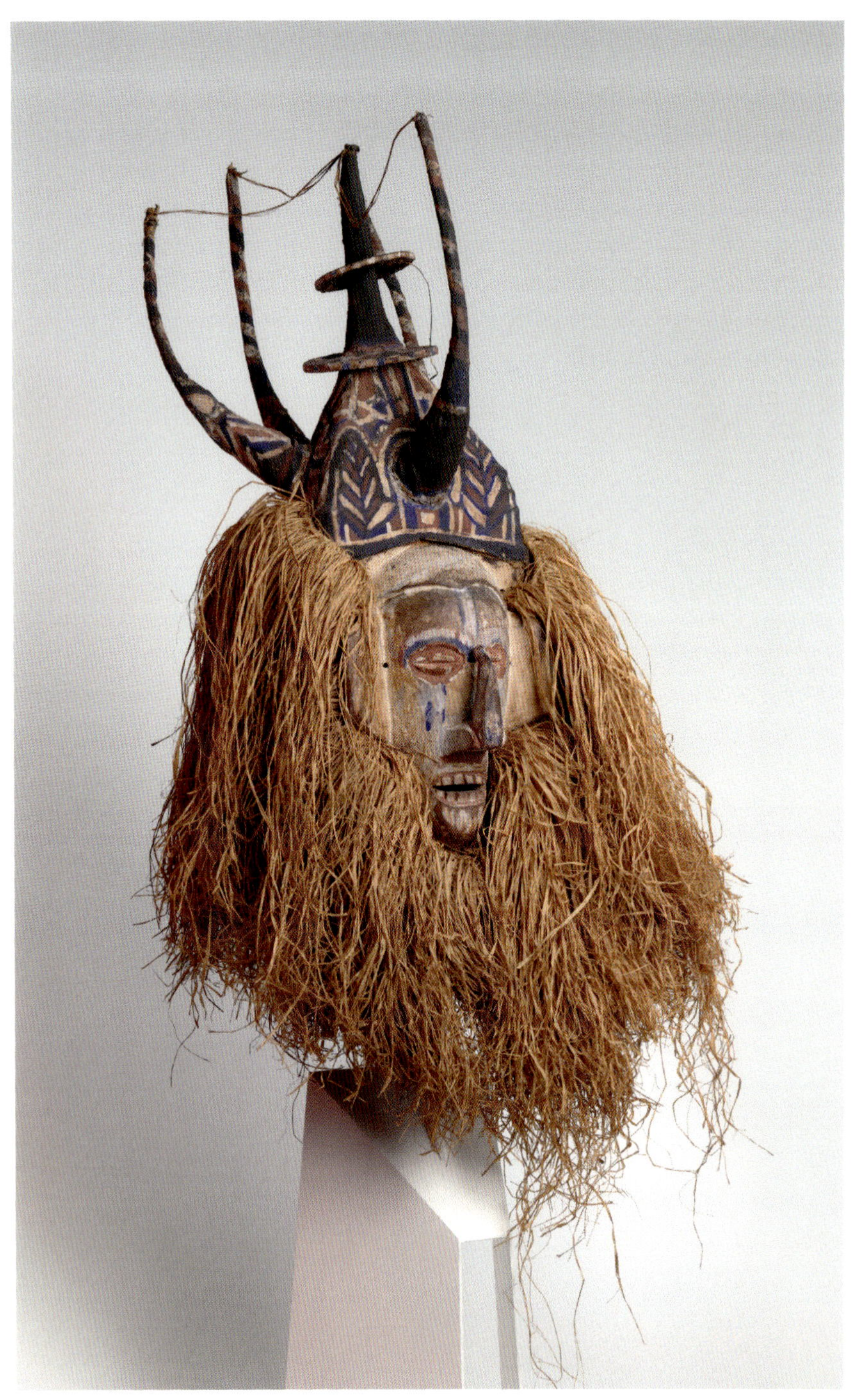

Cat. 26. Yaka artist. Kholuka Mask, 1900s. Painted wood, raffia, and burlap. 40 × 21 × 16 in. Gift of John and Mary Pat Carlen, 1986.352.

Guinea Masks: Baga

Among the Baga in present-day Guinea, masks embody human and animal features. The mask in the museum's collection represents the spirit Kumbaruba (also known as Banda) (cat. 27, p. 44). It has characteristics common among Baga women, like facial scarification, as well as animal elements representing a crocodile's jaws, an antelope's horns, a snake's body, and a chameleon's tail. These symbols provide safeguards in times of uncertainty. Historically, Kumbaruba appeared to privileged elders, and rituals used masks like this to protect them against threats such as animal attacks or malevolent people. Today, the Kumbaruba headdress is danced only for entertainment. The performer, usually a young man, carries the wooden headdress on top of his head, and the large raffia cape covers his face and extends to his knees. The performance is accompanied by drummers playing on giant wooden slit gongs. His choreography invokes the movements of soaring birds, stamping bulls, and undulating serpents. In the most spectacular section of the dance, he goes into a dizzying spin, holding the headdress aloft, then twirling it in a series of figure eights and plunging it to the ground before finally returning the headdress to his head. Baga cultural artworks are not as prevalent in global North museum collections because of the region's isolation in the marshlands of the Guinea coast.[57]

The Makonde of Tanzania and Mozambique

The Makonde of Tanzania and Mozambique are unique in the East African region for their proliferation of mask forms and styles. In contrast to other East African carving traditions, Makonde sculpture has a long history, with precolonial examples in many Western ethnological collections that predate their entry into the modern export market. They are made by sculptors in family groups, who regard themselves as having a deep connection to their work regardless of its intended audience. In the present, Makonde hold fast to markers of identity that have disappeared from many East African countries that are former British colonial territories: Some of them still file their teeth, wear the upper lip plug, and display elaborate facial scarifications. The Makonde have bifurcated their art production, unlike the Yoruba and Senufo, whose precolonial mask and figure genres entered into wider circles of exchange as

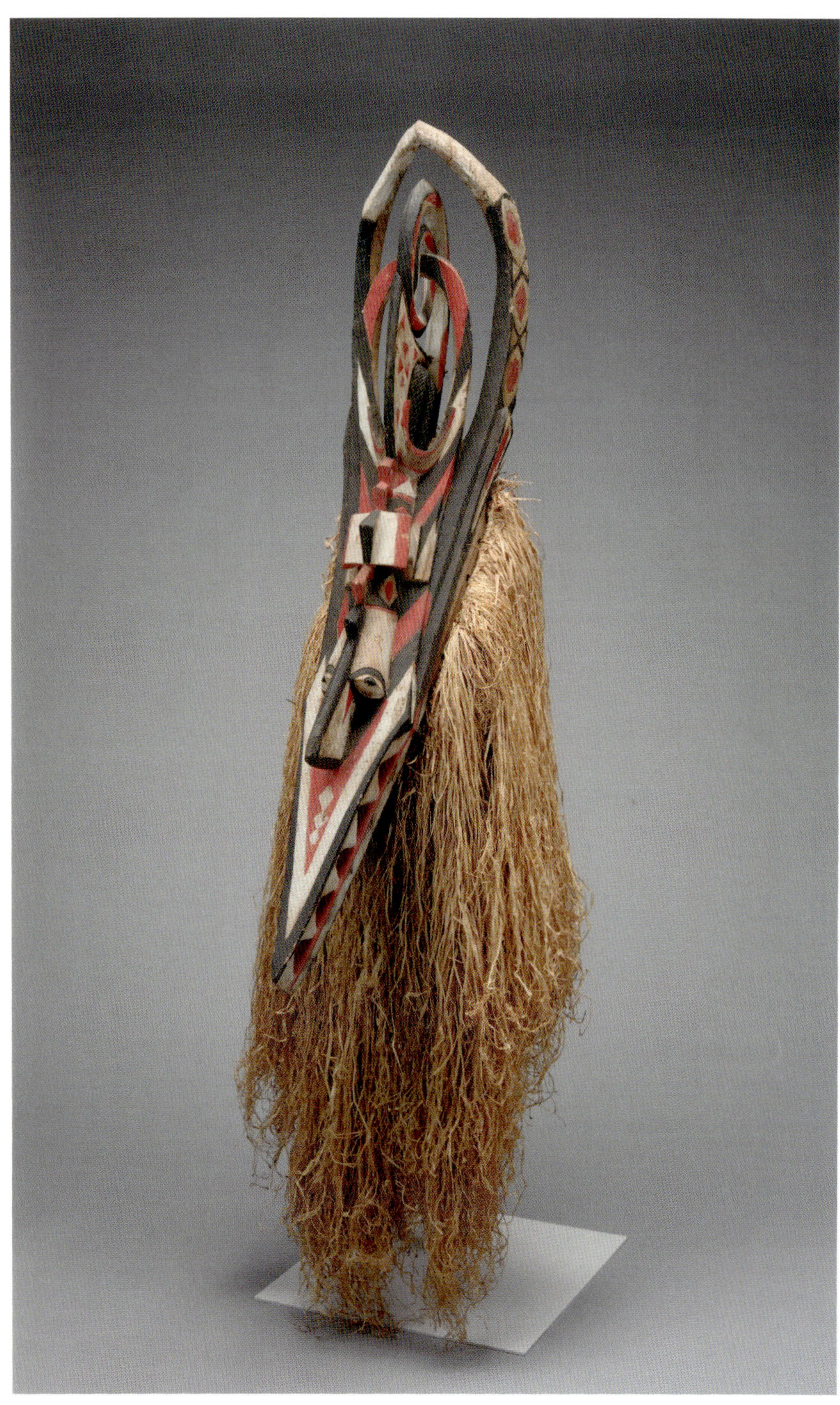

Cat. 27. Baga artist. Kumbaruba Mask, mid-1900s. Painted wood and raffia, 63½ × 14¼ × 11 in.
Native Arts acquisition funds, 1971.665.

commodities. Makonde *mapiko* initiation masks, such as this one, continue to be made and used by the Makonde themselves (cat. 28). This mask entered the museum's collection through an exchange with a gallery specializing in African historical art. Although it was not made for the art market, its provenance does not raise concern that it was acquired illegally by the collector. In contrast, the new genres are made by the same artists for a completely different audience: the art market. This has caused considerable ambivalence in Western art markets because Makonde sculpture does not comfortably fit into either an art or a commodity designation.[58]

The *mapiko* dance, where this mask is worn, is a celebratory part of the rite of passage from puberty to adulthood. The dance is performed in an enclosure, typically under mango trees, where dancers, musicians, and the public come together to celebrate the initiation rite. The dance can also be performed at a community member's funeral or for entertainment purposes.

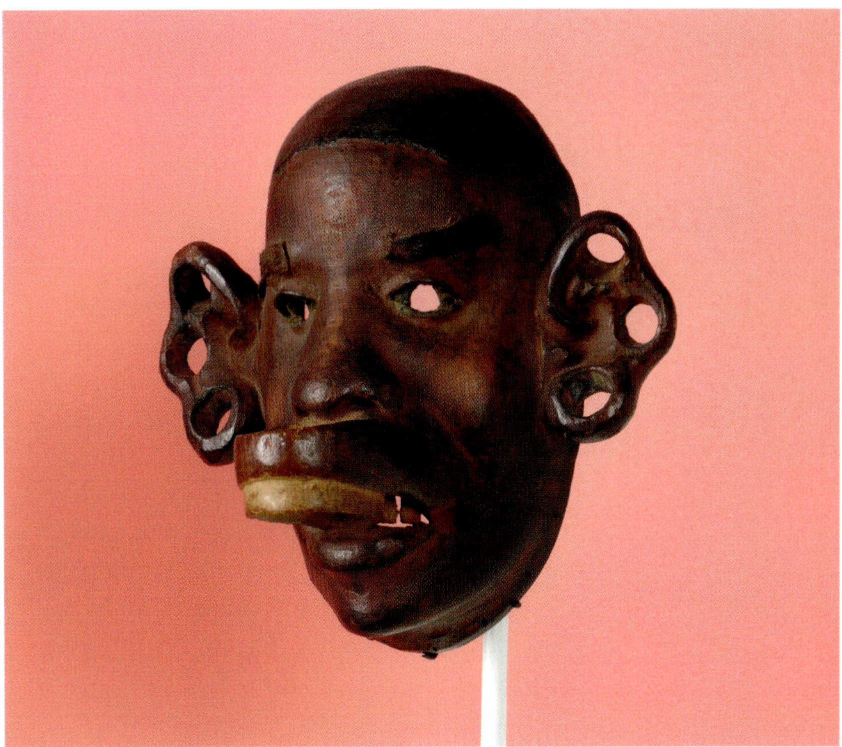

Cat. 28. Makonde artist. *Mapiko* Mask, about 1900. Wood, fur, and fiber, 8½ × 9 × 5 in. Museum exchange with Julius Carlebach, 1960.102.

Ancient Egypt and Morocco: Of Africa but Not In Africa

The Berlin Conference, held between November 1884 and February 1885, was a pivotal meeting of European countries to discuss colonial claims and establish guidelines for the occupation of African territories. Fourteen European nations were represented, including France, Germany, and the United Kingdom. The conference regulated European colonization in Africa, negatively impacting not just Africans but also how people learned about the history of Africa. Within art history, West and Central African art came to be understood as "fetishes" while East and South African art was considered "ethnographic specimens."[59] Additionally, ancient Egyptian art was separated from the rest of Africa, instead becoming the starting point for the narrative of Western civilization. Egyptian culture and art inspired Greek art, which in turn inspired Roman art, culminating in Renaissance art and the modern intellectual world. The rest of African art, on the other hand, was divorced from this narrative of human advancement.[60]

The exclusion of North African art history from the broader history of African ways of life resulted in a lack of connection between the beliefs that Africans have about the afterlife. Communities like the Igbo of Nigeria still hold beliefs about the reincarnation of the soul similar to those of ancient Egyptians, and among the Dogon, in Mali, a funerary ceremony called the *dama* is performed to guide the spirit of the deceased into the next world.[61] The museum's seven-piece wooden boat dates from the Middle Kingdom of ancient Egypt, between 2040 and 1782 BCE (cat. 29). Death was a vital transition rather than an end, and a person's moral conduct during their lifetime, coupled with proper funerary practices, was crucial to ensuring safe passage to the afterlife. Boats like this one held an important place in Egyptian life and mythology. On the one hand, they were the primary form of transportation on the Nile, and on the other hand, they facilitated funerary processions, ferrying someone's soul into the afterlife. This boat was made to carry the soul of the deceased, who was buried with it. Layered with paint, it holds a figure of the deceased, accompanied by two rowers, who likely would have served him in his next life. During excavations of larger tombs of royalty and wealthy Egyptians, archaeologists sometimes unearthed full-size boats.

Daggers, a common tool of war in desert cultures, were also used beyond North Africa, including in the Afar region of Ethiopia, Eritrea, and Djibouti. Further south in eastern Africa, the Maasai and Kikuyu used a simi dagger in battle.[62]

The museum's *koummya*, also spelled *khoumija* or *koumaya*, is a curved dagger of the Imazighen (Berber) peoples in Morocco (cat. 30, p. 48). It was historically used in battle, delivering slashing cuts while also protecting the wielder's backhand. Koummyas are now used as decorative pieces, adding to the uniforms of traditional dancers or worn by a groom as part of the traditional wedding attire. This one was made before 1938 and was purchased as a decorative piece.

From the late nineteenth century, Black communities in the diaspora looked to North Africa, particularly Egypt, as evidence of an undeniably great ancient African culture in an effort to reclaim the identities that were systematically stripped from them through the transatlantic slave trade and continued dehumanization in colonial and American societies.

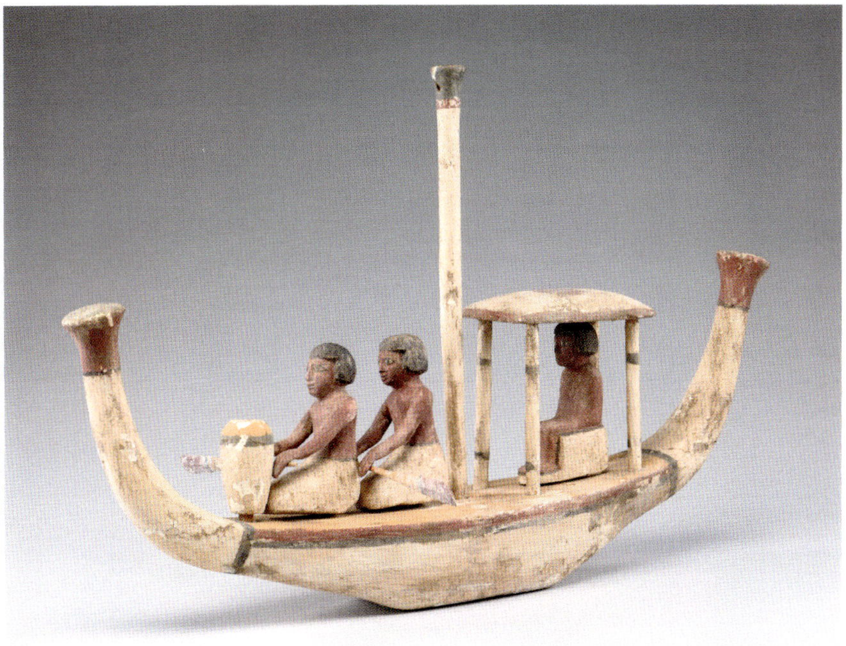

Cat. 29. Egyptian artist. Tomb Soul Boat Model, 1991–1786 BCE. Carved wood, gesso, and pigment, 23 × 11 7⁄8 × 14 1⁄4n. Museum purchase for the Samuel S. Newbury Memorial, 1960.22A-F.

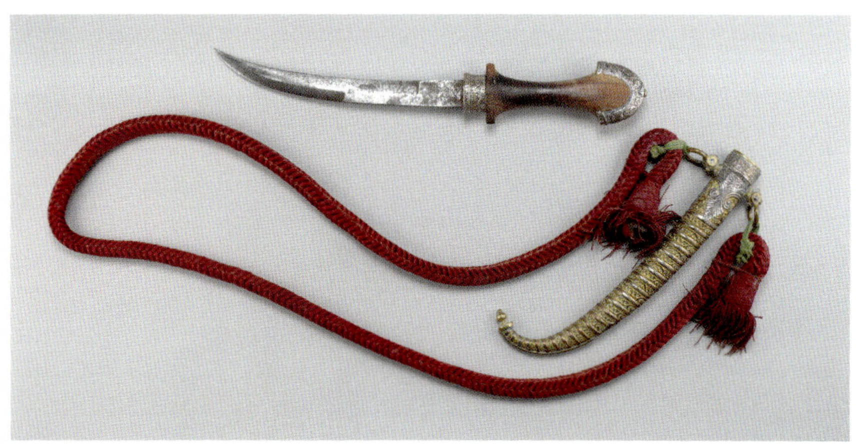

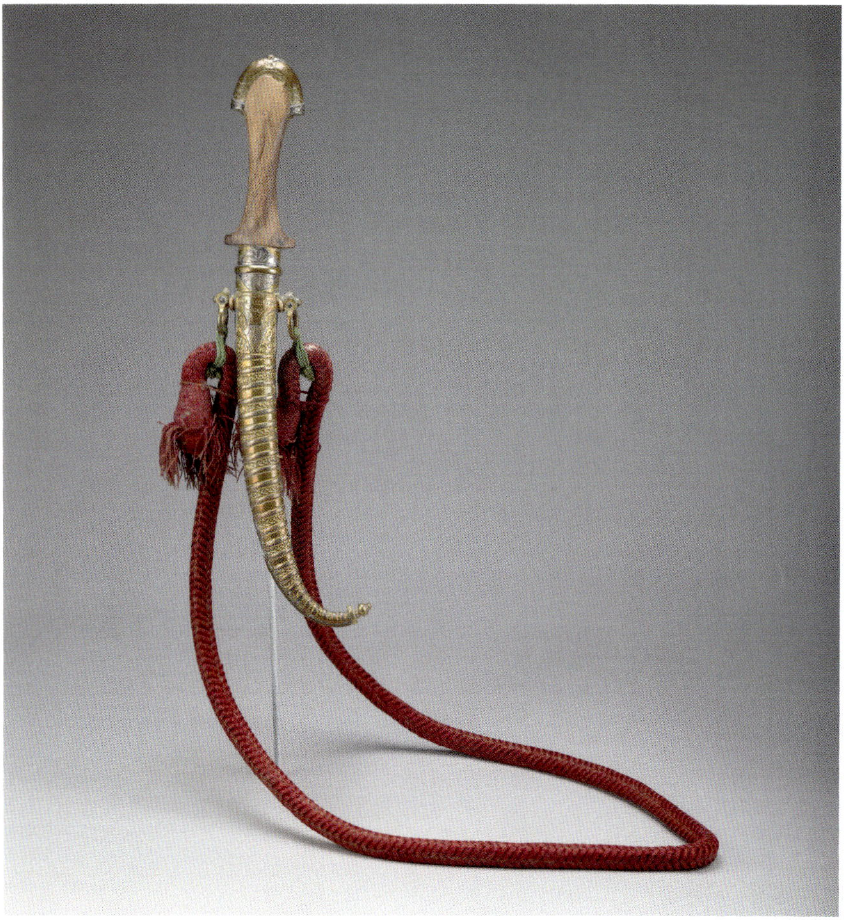

Cat. 30. Imazighen (Berber) artist. *Khoumya* (Decorative Dagger and Sheath), before 1938.
Silver or brass, wood, and wool, 36 × 8 × 2 in. In memory of John A. and Mary Riley, 2022.143A-B.

African Independence and the Postcolonial Moment

In the twentieth century, African activists fighting for freedom from colonial rule found inspiration from Black Americans in the Civil Rights movement. Many Africans and African Americans acknowledged their shared histories of oppression, despite their different contexts. Ghana was the first African country to gain independence in 1957, serving as a beacon for freedom across Africa and in the diaspora. As other African countries followed, Nigeria in 1960, Tanzania in 1961, and Kenya in 1963, these exciting developments inspired many Black American activists to see their struggle in more international terms. Their own fight for civil rights was now in solidarity with anticolonial independence movements worldwide.[63] The afro comb, a shared symbol among Black people around the globe, emerged as a potent symbol of empowerment and resistance (cats. 31 and 32, p. 50). It became synonymous with the struggle for equality and self-determination. Activists marching the streets proudly wore their afros and afro combs to capture the spirit of defiance and solidarity that defined that time, finding collective meaning and hope embodied in the hair adornment.

While the intellectual debates for freedom usually circulated through the literature of African writers, freedom-writing also spilled into art and music. In postcolonial

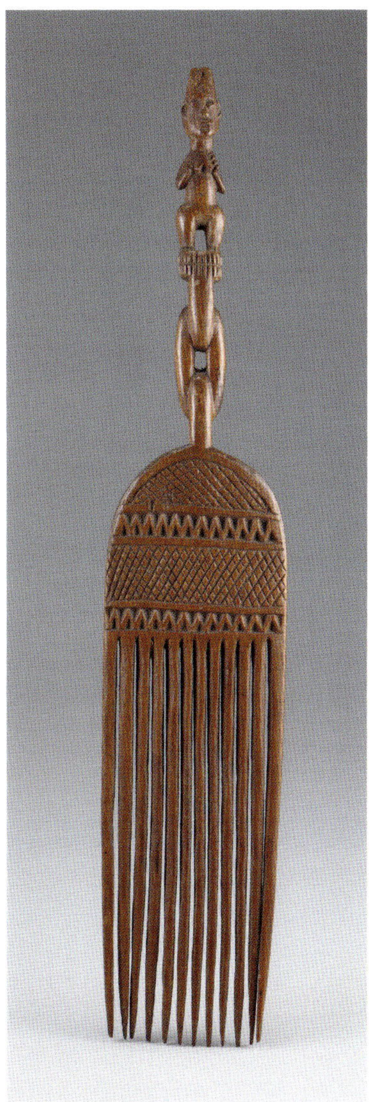

Cat. 31. Nupe artist. Comb with Standing Human Figure, 1800s. Wood, 17 × 3⅝ × ½ in. Gift of Cedric Marks, 1970.813.

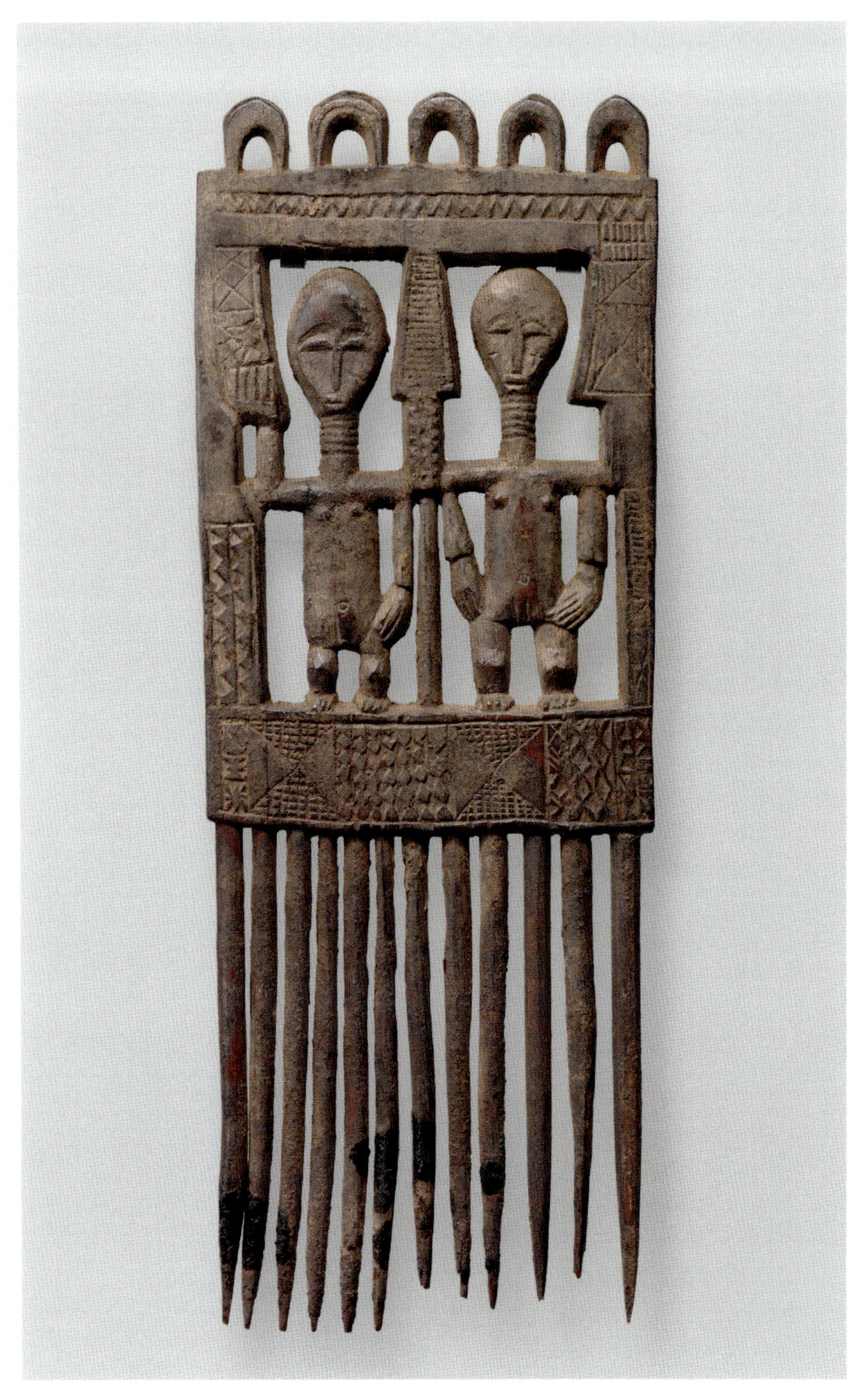

Cat. 32. Ashanti artist. Comb with Two Standing Figures, mid-1900s. Wood, 10¼ × 4 in. Anonymous gift, 2001.1008.

Uganda, this created an inclusive atmosphere for emerging African artists, with many notable artists from a vast region, spanning from Sudan to Zimbabwe, receiving their training at the University of Makerere's School of Art and Design. Students were encouraged to use pictorial narratives for content that had previously resided in oral tradition. The pictorial narrative was rare in Africa before 1900, aside from prehistoric rock art. Today, it is a staple of African art everywhere, from the heroic exploits of the gods to the struggles of everyday life and the chilling allegories of military rule.[64] Sculpture, unable to carry the same complex narrative load as painting, could still thematize both mythic and genre subjects.

When Idi Amin came to power through Uganda's coup d'etat in 1971, much of the creative freedom evaporated. In a very short amount of time, all public criticism was stifled, and the artists who survived (not all did) either went into exile or lived by their wits, evading detection. During that time, expatriates and politically outspoken Ugandans were forced to leave the university. Francis Nnaggenda, a painter, sculptor, and poet, narrowly escaped imprisonment by leaving the country just in time. Nnaggenda is known for his large sculptures in wood and metal that explore the resilience of the human body and spirit in the face of war, violence, and technological advancements. As part of his artistic practice, he incorporates found objects and jagged textures that suggest hints of pain.[65] He also combines techniques from around the world with African traditions, similar to Picasso's cubism. "People tell me my work looks like Picasso, but they have it wrong. It is Picasso who looks like me, like Africa," he says.[66] While in exile, he studied, worked, and taught in Europe, the US, and other African countries before returning to Uganda at the end of Amin's dictatorship in 1978.[67] *Spiritual Messenger* is an abstracted standing human figure with bulging eyes that he made while in Nairobi, Kenya, in 1971 (cat. 52, see p. 83). The mouth is open, its right arm is folded in front, and its hand stretches towards its face. Nnaggenda used welded recycled chunks of metal and old car parts to create a new form.

THE POWER OF THE COMB

Kendall Taylor

Traditional African combs and styling practices are still alive among descendants on the continent and across the globe.[1] In the diaspora of the United States in the 1920s and '30s, Madam C. J. Walker revolutionized how Black American women accessed haircare and styling tools since they had not existed on a commercial level before.[2] In the 1940s and '50s, when segregation was still well underway, Black Americans found solace in barbershops and salons of their own creation.[3] Traditional African combs, later called picks, continued to be a tool for hair as an art medium during the Black Power Movement of the 1960s and '70s.[4] As of 2025, twenty-eight states, including Colorado, signed into law the CROWN (Create a Respectful and Open World for Natural Hair) Act that legally protects hair related to African styles and textures.[5] Unfortunately, this act was necessary due to practices of racially motivated discrimination against such hairstyles in the workplace.[6]

African history details a long practice of hair grooming as a medium of artistic communication.[7] Comb designs are deliberate, communicating identity, family history, and proverbs because in African cultures, the way one's hair is organized may also reflect one's social status, gender, ethnic origin, leadership role, personal taste, or place in the cycle of life.[8] A comb is largely made of softwood, with additional materials like bone, ivory, or metal for wealthier clients.[9] A royal clan may inscribe details on a comb, such as animal designs, gold elements, carvings, and paint[10] that denote their family lineage and status. Combs are specially designed for festivals and ceremonies, such as weddings, burials, or puberty.[11] No detail in the comb-making process is overlooked—even the number of teeth has meaning: For example, in Akan culture, regionally understood as present-day Ghana, seven is a sacred number, thus many combs have a minimum of seven teeth.[12]

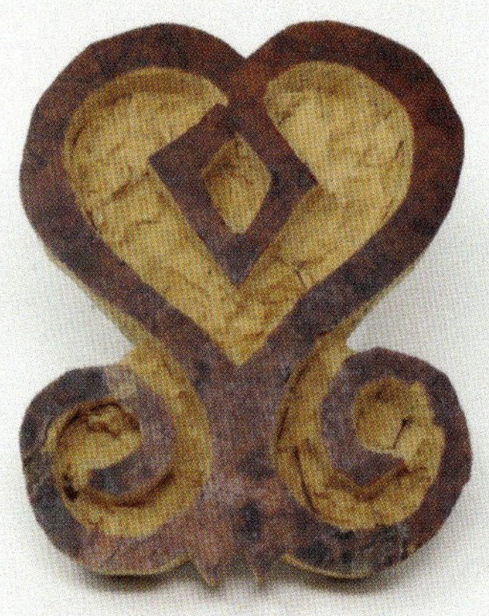

Fig. 1. Adinkra Stamp, late 1900s. Gourd. Textile and Costume Collection, Thomas Jefferson University, Philadelphia, PA. Textile and Costume Collection.

One example of Akan adornment is Sankofa, an Adinkra symbol meaning "go back and fetch it" that can be expressed as a bird looking back at its tail while the body is oriented forward or as a more abstract emblem (fig. 1).[13] The traditional meaning behind the phrase is to encourage looking to the past as a way of moving forward. The Comb with Bird, in the Denver Art Museum collection, can be interpreted as a gift that could be interrupted by the receiver as a reminder to not forget where they come from as they move through life (cat. 33). For Black Americans, African heritage lives in the memory of the ancestors through African symbols that have survived the transatlantic slave trade and have been further curated in the cultural amalgamation of the diaspora. This cultural heritage can be understood as a means of building community that serves as a foundation for social justice movements.[14]

The symbol became important to the development of African studies in the US in the 1970s.[15] During the Black Power movement of that time, scholarship encouraged Africans of the diaspora to "go back and fetch it," indicating to go back and fetch the history and realign the disrupted African history with diasporic culture. In this way, Sankofa became a renewed symbol of revolution in the act of reclaiming cultural memory and heritage.[16]

The functionality of the comb in the act of beautification creates an invaluable tool for revolutionary self-expression. Combs represent the connective historical thread between the African continent and diaspora.

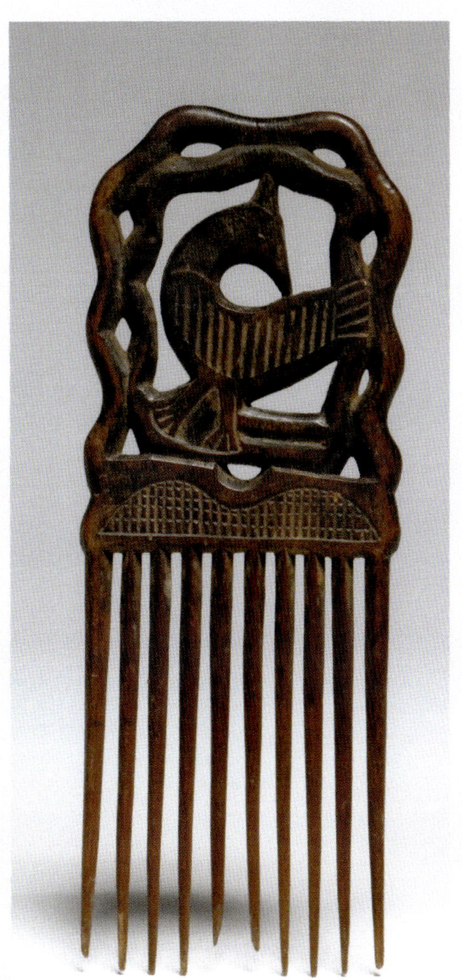

Cat. 33. Akan artist. Comb with Bird, mid-1900s. Wood, 9 × 3½ in. Anonymous gift, 2001.1012.

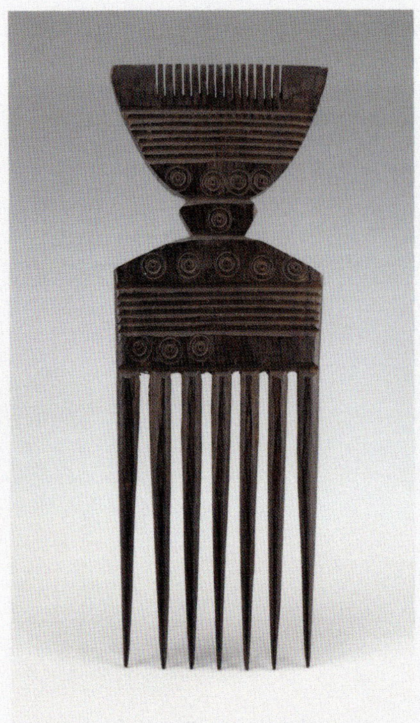

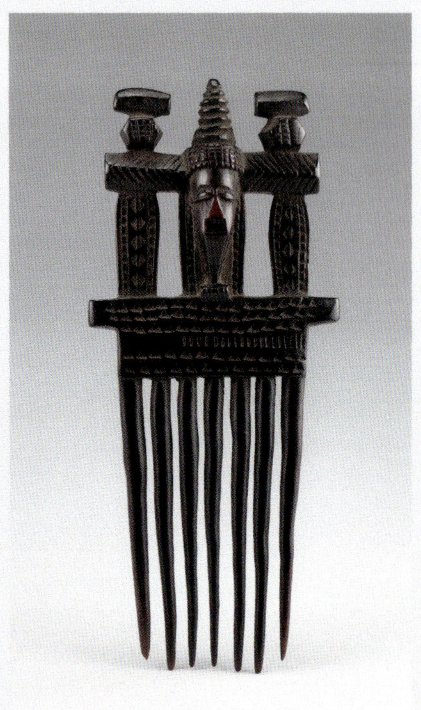

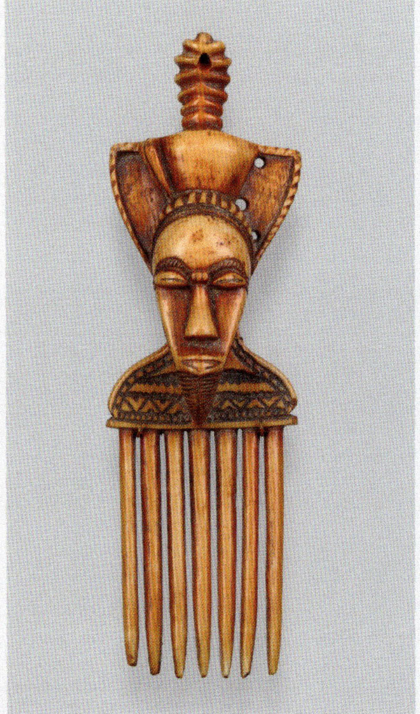

Upper left: Zulu artist. Comb with Toothed Abstract Design, early 1900s. Wood, 6⅝ × 2¼ in. Gift of Leota J. Roberts, 1954.540.

Above: Akan artist. Comb with Head Wearing a Headpiece, likely mid-1900s. Wood, 7½ × 3½ in. Anonymous gift, 2001.1010.

Left: Baule artist. Comb with Bearded Human Face Wearing Headpiece, mid-1900s. Ivory, 7¼ × 2¾ × 1½ in. Anonymous gift, 2001.948.

FACING
Upper left: Luba artist. Comb with Human Face and Beads, mid-1900s. Wood, beads, fiber, and mud, 4¾ × 1½ in. Anonymous gift, 2001.997.

Upper right: Akan artist. Comb with Bird's Head, mid-1900s. Ivory and metal, 4½ × 1¾ in. Anonymous gift, 2001.1025.

Lower left: Dogon artist. Hairpin with Seated Figures, early 1900s. Metal, 10¼ × ¾ × ½ in. Anonymous gift, 2001.1021.

Lower right: Swahili artist. Comb with Toothed Abstract Design, early 1900s. Ebony, 9½ × 3½ in. Native Arts acquisition funds, 1949.4198.

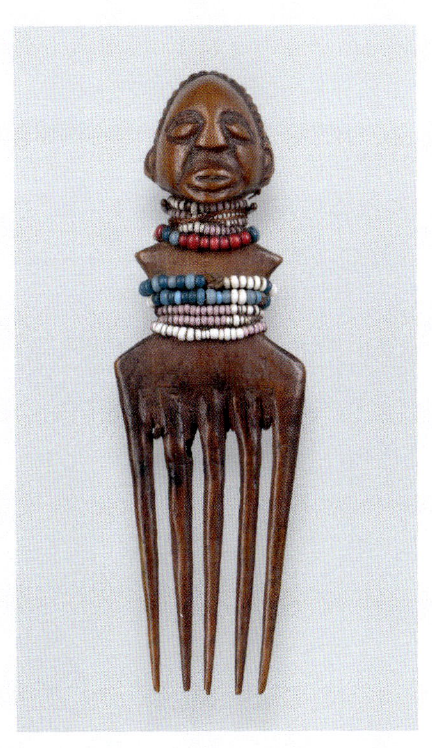
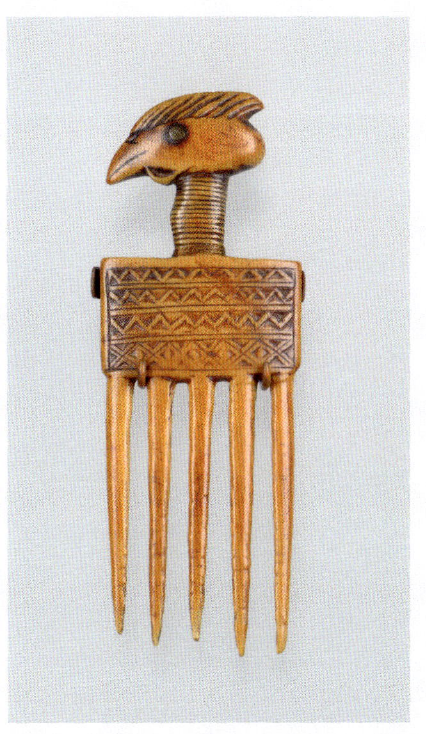
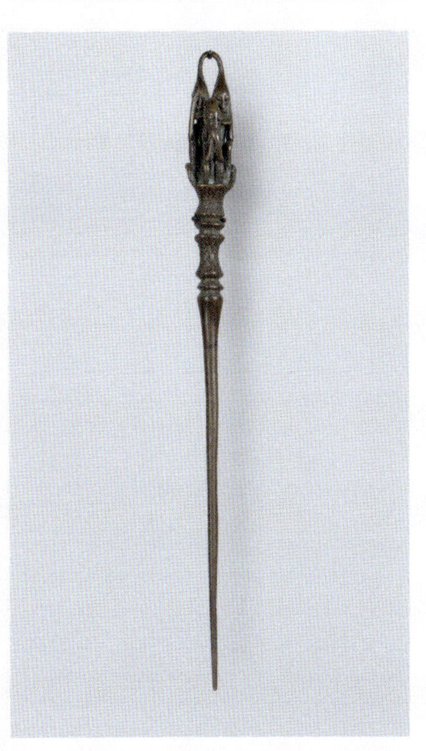
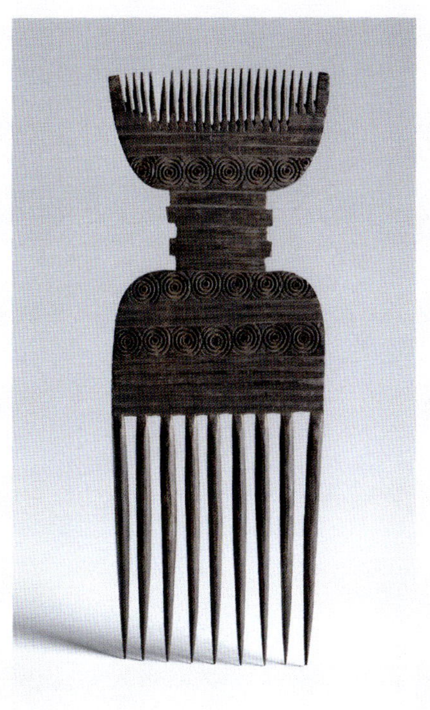

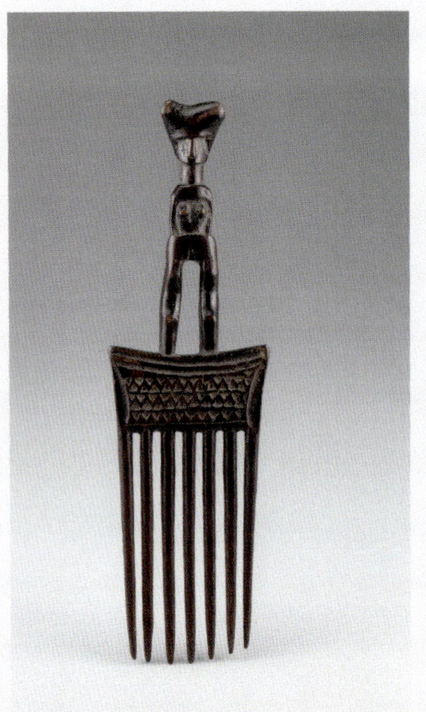

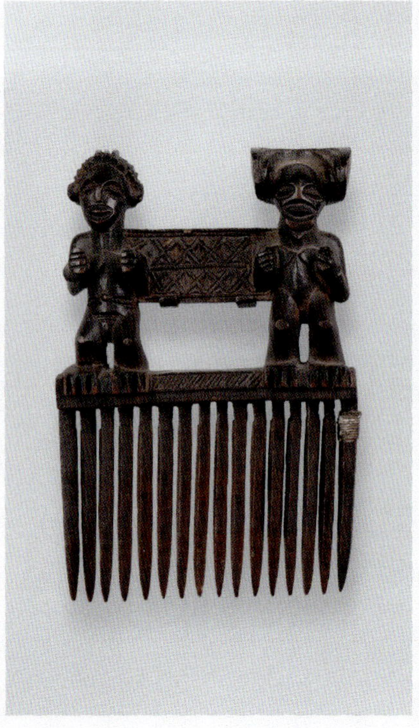

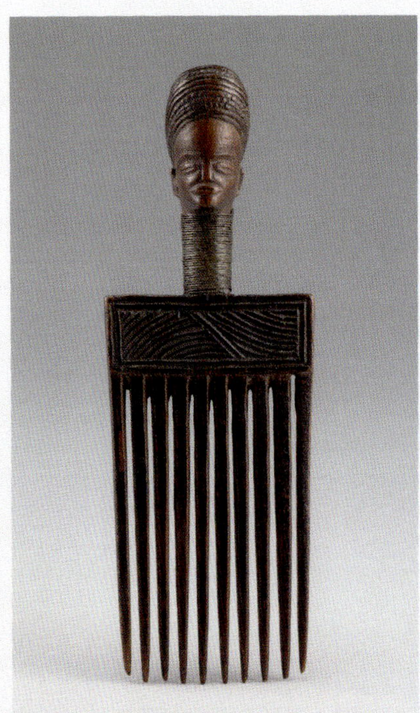

Top left: Baule artist. Comb with Standing Figure, early 1900s. Wood, 9¾ × 3 in. Anonymous gift, 2001.1011.

Top right: Chokwe artist. Comb with Man and Woman Figures, mid-1900s. Painted wood and fiber, 6¼ × 4½ × 1½ in. Anonymous gift, 2001.1004.

Left: Chokwe artist. Comb with Human Face, about 1815–1960. Metal and wood, 6½ × 2½ in. Anonymous gift, 2001.1007.

Facing: Baule artist. Comb with Elongated Human Face, likely mid-1900s. Wood, 7¼ × 1¾ in. Anonymous gift, 2001.1013.

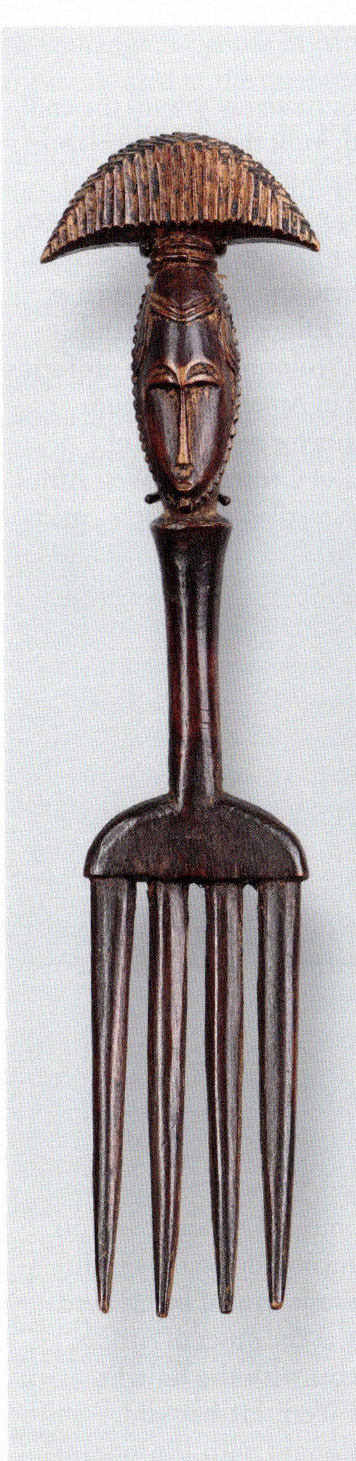

[1] Roy Sieber and Frank Herreman, "Hair in African Art and Culture," *African Arts* 33, no. 3 (2000): 55–96.

[2] Susannah Walker, *Style and Status: Selling Beauty to African American Women, 1920–1975,* (University Press of Kentucky, 2007), 47–84.

[3] Quincy T. Mills, *Cutting Along the Color Line: Black Barbers and Barber Shops in America,* (University of Pennsylvania Press, 2013), 216–48.

[4] Susannah Walker, *Style and Status*, 169–204.

[5] "About," The Official CROWN Act, accessed November 29, 2025, https://www.thecrownact.com/about; Britney Pitts, "'Uneasy Lies the Head That Wears a Crown': A Critical Race Analysis of the CROWN Act," *Journal of Black Studies* 52, no. 7, (2021): 716–35.

[6] Ibid.

[7] Sieber and Herreman, "Hair in African Art and Culture," 55–96.

[8] Ibid.

[9] Janet Adwoa Antiri, "Akan Combs," *African Arts* 8, no. 1 (1974): 32.

[10] Ibid.

[11] Erik R. Seeman, "Reassessing the 'Sankofa Symbol' in New York's African Burial Ground," *The William and Mary Quarterly* 67, no. 1 (2010): 101–22.

[12] Antiri, "Akan Combs," 33.

[13] Christel N. Temple, "The Emergence of Sankofa Practice in the United States: A Modern History," *Journal of Black Studies* 41, no. 1 (2010): 127–50.

[14] Erin Linn-Tynen, "Reclaiming the Past as a Matter of Social Justice: African American Heritage, Representation, and Identity in the United States," in *Critical Perspectives on Cultural Memory and Heritage: Construction, Transformation, and Destruction*, ed. Veysel Apaydin (UCL Press, 2020), 255–68.

[15] Abdul Alkalimat, *The History of Black Studies* (Pluto Press, 2021), 101–27.

[16] Temple, "The Emergence of Sankofa Practice in the United States," 127–50; Walter Johnson and David Brion Davis, "Introduction: The Future Store," in *The Chattel Principle: Internal Slave Trades in the A mericas*, ed. Walter Johnson (Yale University Press, 2004), 1–31; Stephanie Mitchem, "Sankofa: Black Theologies," *CrossCurrents* 50, no. 1/2 (2000): 177–84.

triptych *The Garden of Earthly Delights* (1490–1500, Prado Museum) (cat. 35). Bosch's piece features the color pink to depict a theatrical space where heaven, earth, and hell intersect. Ndzube uses pink to depict a world where otherworldly creatures struggle for power and freedom. The figures in The Bloom of the Corpse Flower sit between the poles of mythology and realism, remembering South Africa's recent violent past while also mythologizing the agency of Black South Africans. The underlying tale becomes a metaphor for colonialism and post-apartheid South Africa, inviting the viewer to reflect on how resilience, freedom, conflict, and tension permeate Black worlds long after independence from colonial rule.[70] As he has said of this series, which was presented in his first US solo museum exhibition, held at the Denver Art Museum in 2021, "I was creating a world where I am in charge. A world where I can celebrate how Black South Africans have held on to their cultures showing a very strong element of resilience."[71]

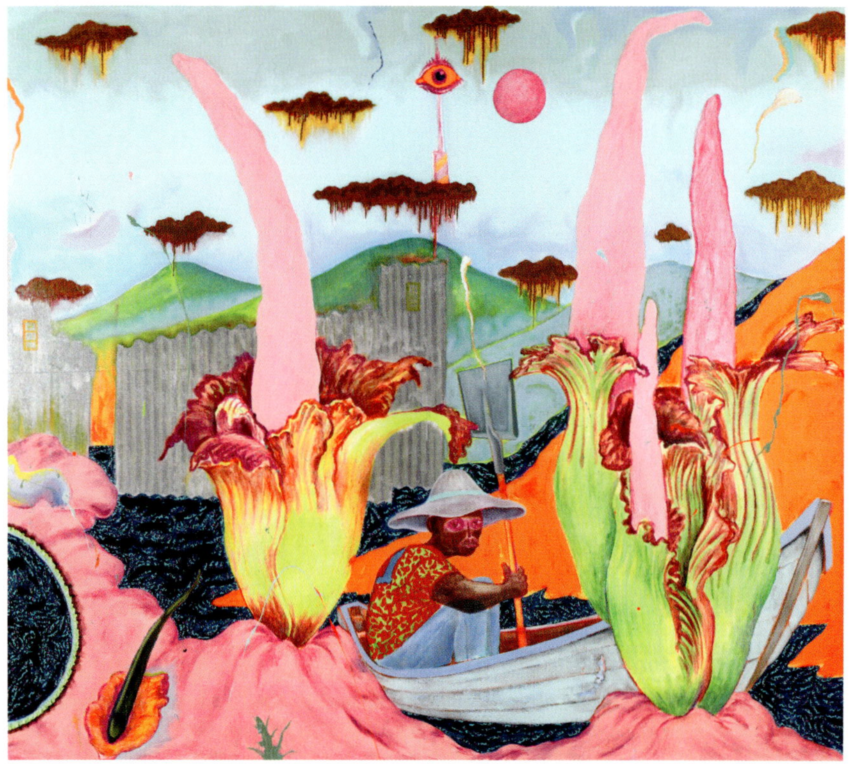

Cat.35. Simphiwe Ndzube (South African, born 1990), ***The Bloom of the Corpse Flower***, 2020. Mixed media on canvas, 95 ×79 in. Funds from the Contemporary Collectors' Circle with additional support from Vicki and Kent Logan, Catherine Dews Edwards and Philip Edwards, Craig Ponzio, Ellen and Morris Susman, and Bryon Adinoff and Trish Holland, 2021.37.

Alioune Diagne, who premiered at Senegal's inaugural pavilion at the Venice Biennale in 2024, creates figurative scenes from countless tiny, unique elements that form remarkably complex compositions depicting daily experiences in Senegal. His unique approach draws from his impressionist artistic training in Paris but expands into a new style he calls "figuro-abstro." It is a technique resembling calligraphy and pointillism, which he developed in 2013 after his grandfather, a Quranic master, died. Diagne uses this figurative language to express what he cannot say with words, forming remarkably complex compositions. The Denver Art Museum was the first American museum to acquire one of Diagne's works, an oil painting on canvas titled *Jeune Marchand Ambulant (The Young Street Vendor)* (cat. 36). The painting transports the viewer into a dense Senegalese market scene. The movement at the heart of the painting evokes the life of the street vendors who are forced to travel far and wide to sell their wares, often in extremely precarious conditions. Through the figure of the street vendor constantly on the move, Diagne echoes his childhood, which was marked by months of solitary walking through the Sine-Saloum region in search of his father, himself perpetually on the move to provide for his family.

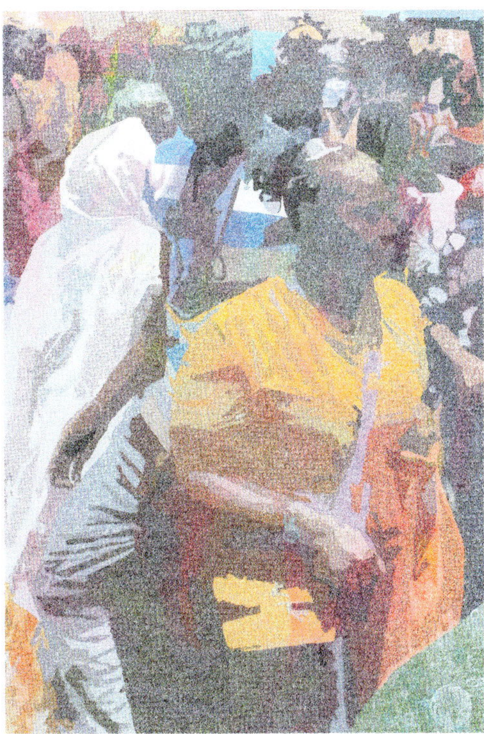

Cat. 36. Alioune Diagne (Senegalese, born 1985), *Jeune Marchand Ambulant* (*The Young Street Vendor*), 2022. Oil paint on canvas, 118⅛ × 78 ¾ in. Purchased with Black Arts Collective funds from U.S. Bank, Craig Ponzio, Daniel and Saron Yohannes, Aminata and Hamidou Dia, Maude Lofton, Geta and Janice Asfaw, Wole Bakare, Javon Brame, Denise Burgess, Chris and Lu Law, Tamara and Damani Leech, Tina Walls, Letarik Amare, Abasi and Toni Baruti, Jayde and Delroy Gill, Paula Hanson, James and Wendy Holmes, Brooke and Julien McClean, Cleo Parker Robinson, Senga Nengudi, Stephanie and Floyd Rance, Ellen Anderman and James C. Donaldson, and Donna and Steve Good, 2024.433.

Cheick Diallo, an architect and designer from Mali, uses a variety of salvaged materials, including steel, plastic, rubber, wood, and clay in his work. He prefers to use recycled objects, tying into the African tradition of reusing materials. He searches for local sources and finds novel applications in his designs. For example, in *M'be yan II (I'm Here)*, he incorporates salvaged steel into rectangles of varying sizes and color, forming a tilted cube that is a chair (cat. 37). The shape of the chair and the salvaged materials challenge common perceptions of African design by combining the centuries-old craft of chair carving with the contemporary sensibility of recycling steel.

Hamed Ouattara also seeks to transform everyday materials left behind. He focuses on materials left behind from the continuing high levels of violence by nonstate armed groups and military operations in Burkina Faso. Despite a shortage of tools, frequent power outages, and the ongoing disruptions of civil war, he works with a team of local

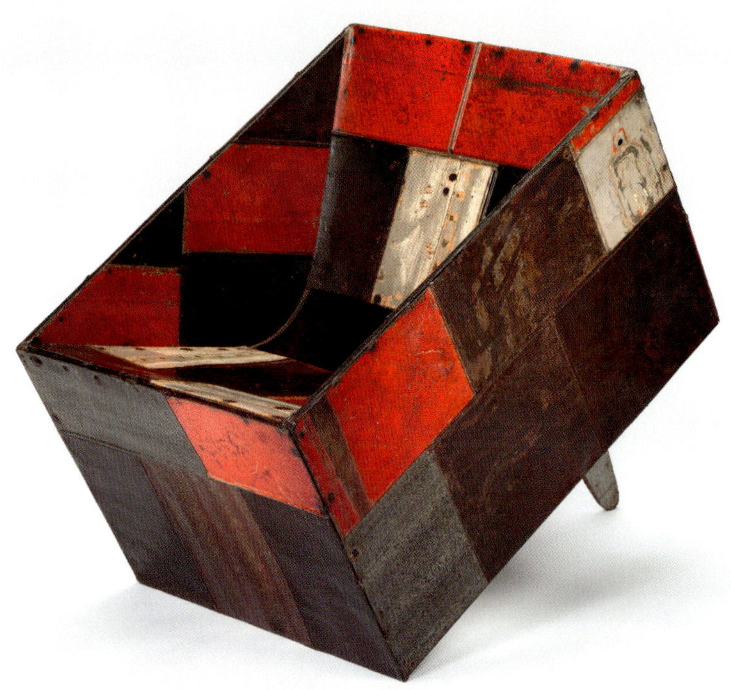

Cat. 37. Cheick Diallo (Malian, born 1960). *M'be yan II (I'm Here)*, 2018. Reclaimed steel, 32 × 24 × 41 in. Funds from the Architecture and Design Collectors' Council, with additional support from Nancy Leprino, 2023.79.

artisans to transform mundane found objects into functional chairs, cabinets, and tables, while ensuring each piece retains its original story, down to the peeling surfaces, as seen in *Indigola Cabinet* (cat. 38). He also reinterprets traditional African patterns with brilliant colors. Each piece, with its worn patina, draws attention to its former life and the stories it still carries.

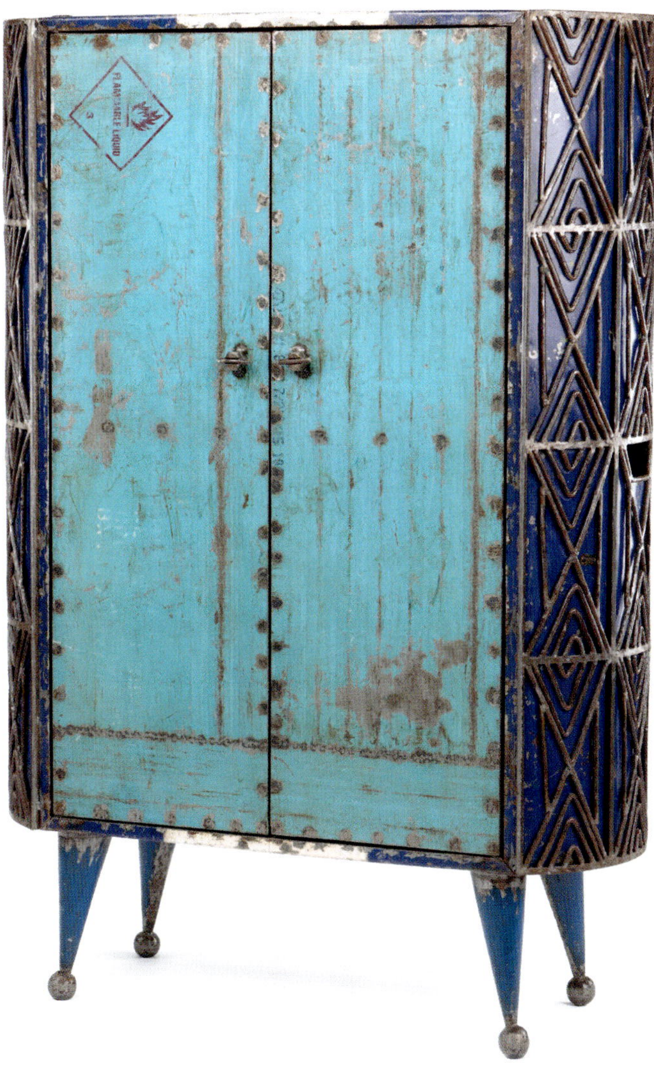

Cat. 38. Hamed Ouattara (Burkinabé, born 1971). *Indigola Cabinet*, 2014. Reclaimed oil drums, 48 × 34 × 13⅛ in. Funds from the Architecture and Design Collectors' Council, with additional support from Nancy Leprino, 2023.204.

For Andile Dyalvane, clay or *umhlaba* (mother earth) is his preferred medium. He uses it as a tool to chronicle his life, channel memory, and honor his Xhosa ancestors while expressing aspirations for the present. Clay is an energetic link to his past, present, and future. *iKhaya (Home)* (cat. 39) is a hand-coiled ceramic seat made from terracotta clay. It is part of a series of Dyalvane's that deploys nearly two hundred unique symbols that denote important words in everyday Xhosa life. The deep incisions on the sides of the chair are inspired by Xhosa and African traditions of body scarification and reflect Dyalvane's commitment to preserving Xhosa knowledge.

Merikokeb Berhanu is absorbed by questions of life, death, and the human condition. Drawing inspiration from nature, she uses colors and shapes to express what cannot be communicated with words, as in *Untitled LXX* (cat. 40, p. 66), which debuted in 2022 at the Venice Biennale. She tries to capture the feelings and emotions that have accompanied her through the different stages of her life. Her artworks are not about specific moments in time and place; rather, they are situated somewhere between the conscious and the subconscious.

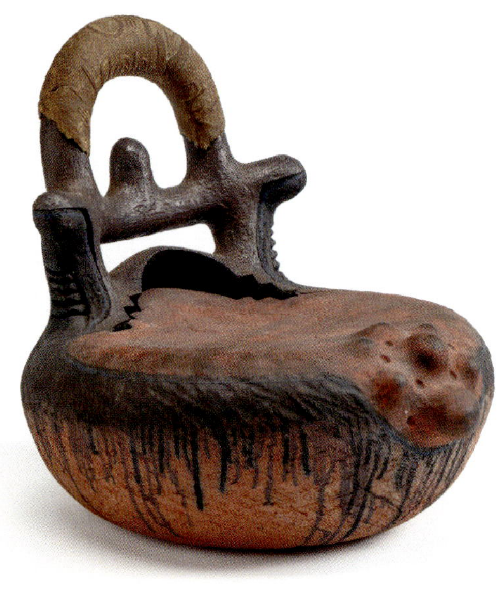

Cat.39. Andile Dyalvane (South African, born 1978). *iKhaya (Home)*, 2020. Ceramic (terracotta), 24½ × 25 × 26 in. Funds from the Architecture and Design Collectors' Council, 2021.120.

ARTIST'S REFLECTION
Merikokeb Berhanu

Syokau Mutonga: What experiences, environments, or encounters consistently spark new ideas in your work?

Merikokeb Berhanu: Much of my inspiration comes from the natural world and from noticing how similar patterns repeat from the smallest to the largest scales of life. I am fascinated by the echo between micro-life (cells, seeds, embryos) and macro-life (landscapes, herds, and human communities). In *Untitled LXX* those resonances appear as ambiguous shapes in the form of cows, cellular forms, or other life-bearing structures (cat. 40, p. 66).

Over the last several years I have also been thinking about human design and the objects we surround ourselves with, such as the synthetic patterns of circuitry, microchips, and other technological diagrams, and how those forms now sit alongside organic ones in our environment. I began to weave circuit-board motifs into my paintings as a way to reflect on this tension: Technology's geometric language sits next to the softer, repeating geometry of seeds and cells so that the canvas becomes a place where nature and the machine converse. These formal juxtapositions are part of a broader inquiry in my work into rapid urbanization and the ways modern life has reshaped our relationship to the living world. In *Untitled LXX*, you will notice hints of synthetic, circuit-like structure threaded through the more natural elements of the composition. I use those marks not to reject technology but to ask viewers to look closely at how the technological and the natural now mirror, disrupt, and inform one another.

Syokau Mutonga: What relationship do you hope to create between your work and those who experience it?

Merikokeb Berhanu: I hope for my paintings to open a contemplative space, where viewers can sense both the intimacy of their own emotions and their connection to something larger. I do not prescribe a single meaning. Instead, I invite people to pause, to look closely, and to listen to what arises in them as they encounter the work. My practice itself is deeply meditative; the act of layering forms and rhythms on canvas is a way of attuning to the spiritual connections that link all living things. In a museum like the Denver Art Museum, where diverse traditions and perspectives are gathered, I hope *Untitled LXX* serves as a reminder of this quiet power of reflection. Even amidst complexity, there is room for stillness, imagination, and renewal.

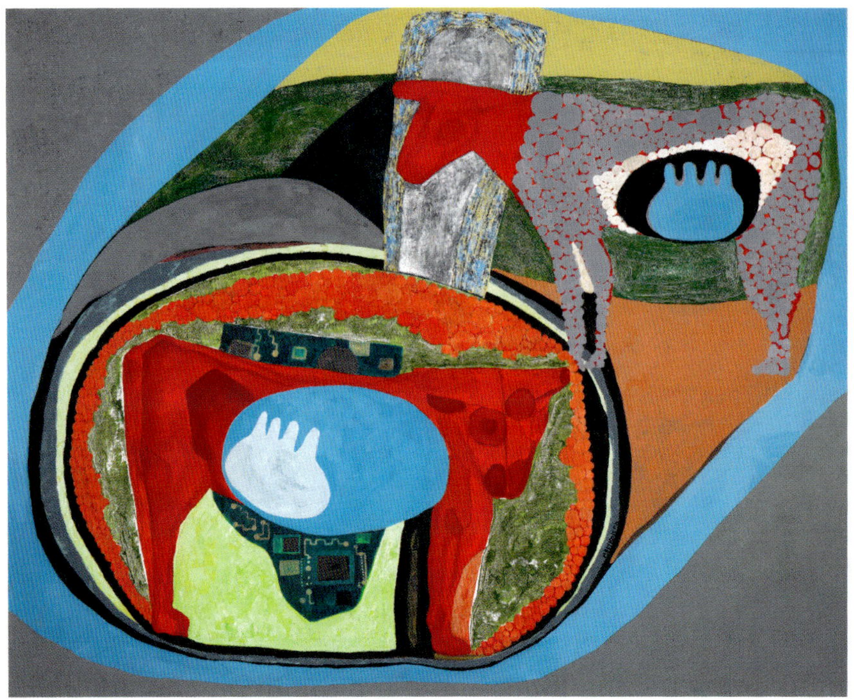

Cat. 40. Merikokeb Berhanu (Ethiopian, born 1977). *Untitled LXX*, 2021. Acrylic on canvas, 48 × 60⅛ in. Funds, by exchange, from John and Mary Pat Carlen, James P. Economos, Jerome Furman, and Dr. E. E. McKeown, 2022.338.

Black Diaspora Art

Going beyond the African continent, Black diasporic art reveals how the tapestries of our shared humanity are woven in colors of difference and diversity. It celebrates the shared Black experience, regardless of place: All Black people are children of histories punctuated by white men and divided by the transatlantic slave trade and the "Scramble for Africa" in Berlin. It reveals the deeper historical contexts and networks of a complex and underrepresented genealogy stemming from African and Black modernities.[72] This is not meant to deny the brutality and cynicism that still characterizes encounters between people and nations. It is intended to show how Black people continue to create ways of being in the world that reject fixed identities. The French writer and poet Édouard Glissant (1928–2011) depicted ongoing renewal through the metaphor of a person on a beach who is constantly repositioning themselves in relation to the moving wave.

Black art within art history is essential to our understanding of the modern world, as it serves both as a perspective and as a developing part of global history. Black artists have created beauty where the Western canon has sought to erase them. Their art reminds us that the processes of mixing and interlacing cultures, peoples, and nations are irreversible.[73] From this mixing and interlacing, a new relational ethic is emerging: restitutionary work that challenges our common consciousness and rebuilds a world where humanity is restored to those who have historically been subjected to processes of abstraction and objectification.

During the late Spanish colonial period in Venezuela, the descendants of freed enslaved Africans ascended the social ladder by participating in craft guilds that had previously been exclusively reserved for people of European descent. Raphael Ochoa's work presents a complex world of race relations and art production at that time. Little is known about the artist, other than that he was a *pardo* (Black person), "Maestro de Pintor" (master painter), and gilder. His painting *Portrait of Don José Bernardo de Asteguieta y Díaz de Sarralde* is signed and dated on the reverse with a large inscription inside a rectangular cartouche: "Rafael Ochoa, *de calidad Negro: lo hizo en* Caracas *Año 1793*" (Rafael Ochoa, of Negro quality: he did it in Caracas, year 1793) (cat. 41, p. 68). This makes clear that Ochoa presented himself as a Black artist—an exceptional artistic statement during the colonial era, given the history of racism at the time. This is the only known signed portrait by Ochoa and one of the few surviving portraits of colonial Venezuela.

In North America, Grafton Tyler Brown is among the few Black Americans who established a career as a professional artist during the nineteenth century. However, in stark contrast to Ochoa, he, for much of his life, and especially after his move to San Francisco in 1860, passed as white among many of his peers and patrons. During a time of extreme racial prejudice throughout the country, this status, which he appears to have passively and actively cultivated, may have helped him succeed in a notoriously exclusionary field. He was born to free Black parents in Pennsylvania but moved west in 1858, eventually running a lithography business. During his painting career, he produced a range of representations of the American West, many of which he sold to tourists traveling along the Northern

Pacific Railway. These included views of Yellowstone National Park, such as *Castle Geyser, Yellowstone* (cat. 42). Using a low horizon line of darkened forest, Brown emphasized the height and brilliance of the erupting geyser. It is delicately painted, with careful textural and tonal differences between stone, spray, forest, and sky.

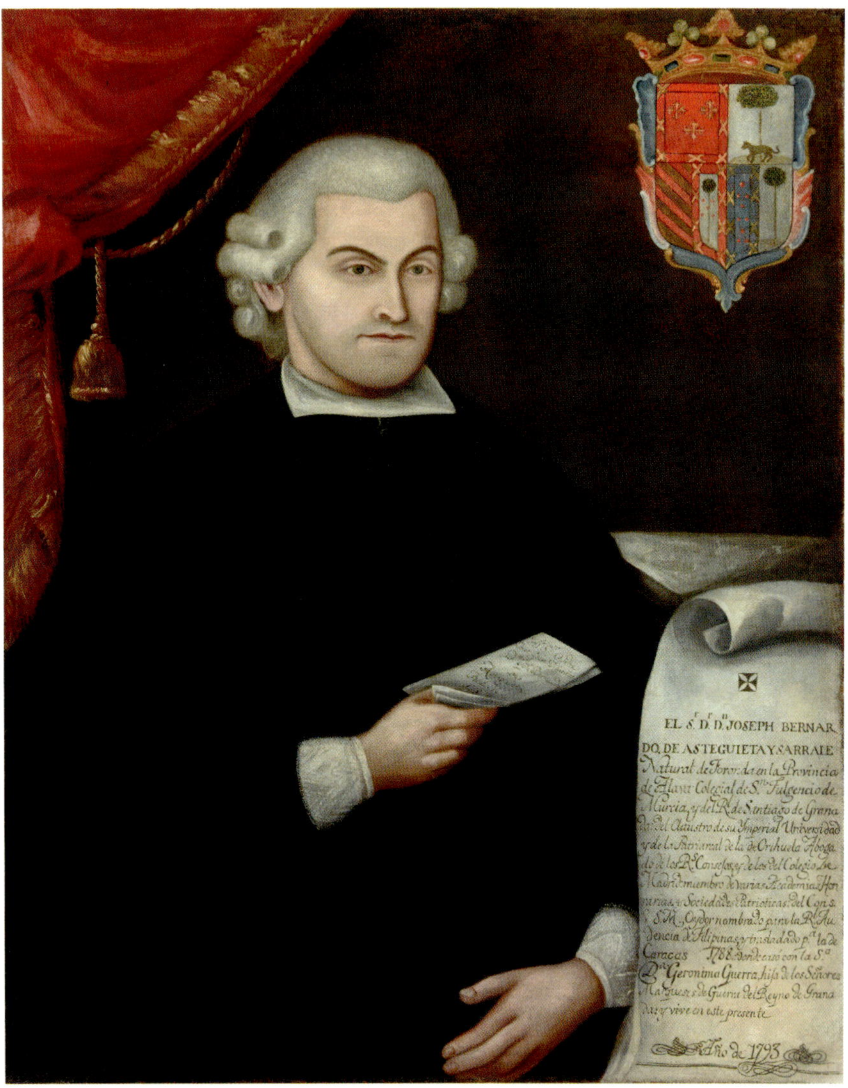

Cat. 41. Rafael Ochoa (Venezuelan, active 1787–1809). *Portrait of Don José Bernardo de Asteguieta y Díaz de Sarralde (1749–1812)*, 1793. Oil on canvas, 39½ × 31⅞ in. Gift of Carl Patterson in honor of Christoph Heinrich, 2017.96.

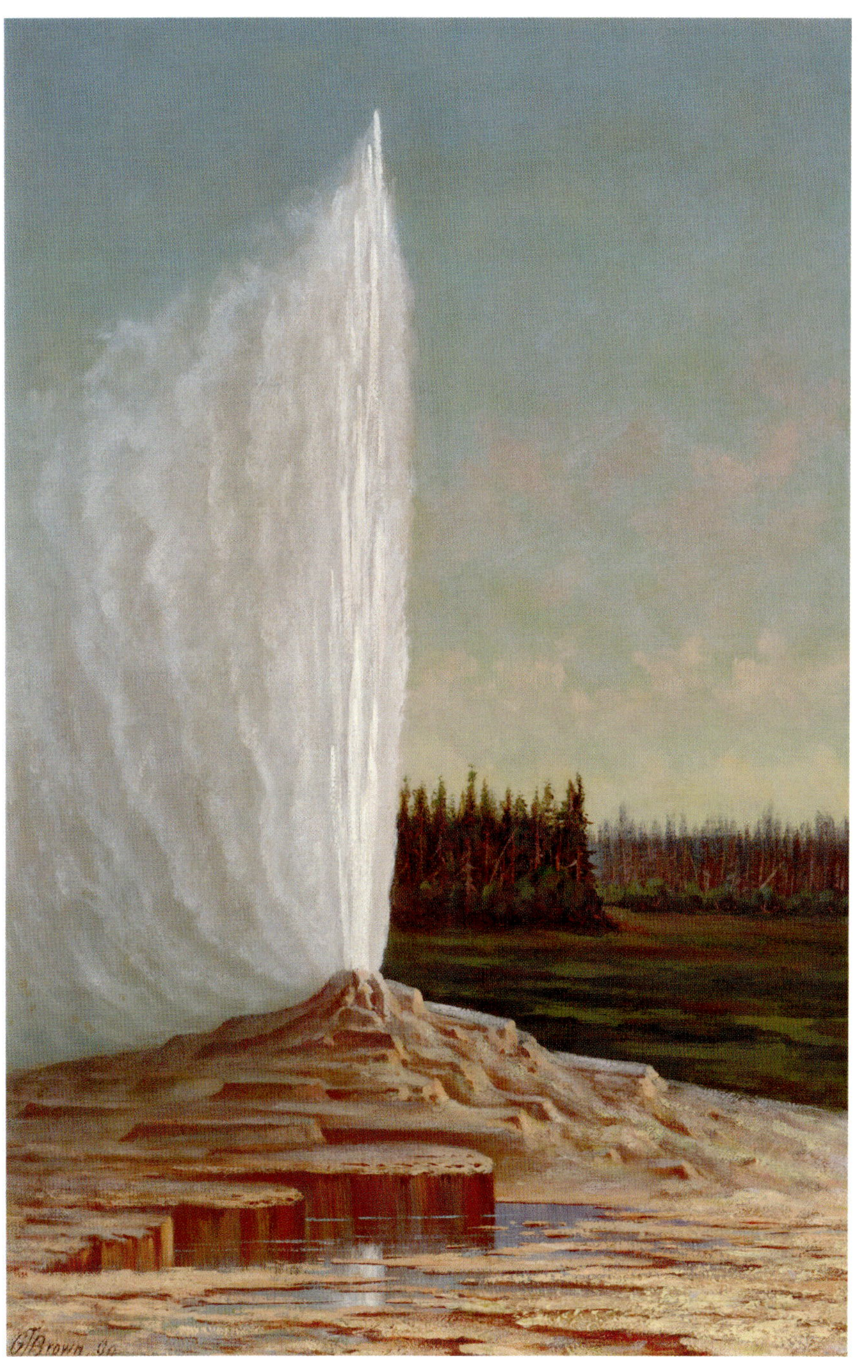

Cat. 42. Grafton Tyler Brown (American, 1841–1918). *Castle Geyser, Yellowstone*, 1890. Oil on canvas, 21⅛ × 14⅜ in. The William Sr. and Dorothy Harmsen Collection at the Denver Art Museum, by exchange, 2020.657.

One hundred years later, Amoako Boafo mines his experience as a Ghanaian artist living and working between Africa and Europe. His work celebrates beauty, confidence, and joy through thickly painted portraits of Black people, such as *Pink Astilbe* (see p. 7). His contemplative and unguarded paintings highlight Black radical joy, where people are not limited to seeing themselves in relation to oppression, even if it is very much a part of the Black diasporic narrative.[74] In *Pink Astilbe*, Boafo depicts this joy through the woman's confident gaze as she unapologetically owns the body and space she inhabits.

Phumelele Tshabalala also paints Black bodies but more directly addresses politicized issues that reflect on his personal experiences and encounters. His works comment on the sociopolitical situation of Black people in post-apartheid South Africa and explores how those reverberations resonate in global discourses. His work celebrates Black agency. For example, in *A monument to the iS'pantsula as mama feeds the community*, he paints the iS'pantsula dance (cat. 43). It is a fusion of Sotho Mqaquanga dance and Kwaito music, featuring a fast-step street dance choreographed by a troupe of men. It was developed in the 1950s, when apartheid restricted the movement of Black South Africans. The dance, with its ritualized, rhythmic movement was a reclaiming of free motion.

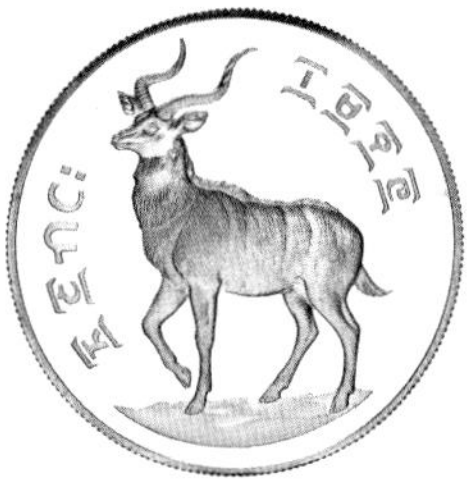

Artists of the diaspora also investigate Blackness through design. Jomo Tariku articulates a new language of contemporary African-themed furniture. As a young boy growing up in Ethiopia, Tariku spent his summers at a local furniture builder. In 2017, he launched his own company in Virginia, where he creates furniture that combines his personal experiences of Africa's diverse cultures, architecture, traditional furniture, landscapes, and wildlife. His *Nyala Chair*, for instance, is inspired by the male mountain nyala, a spiral-horned antelope found in Ethiopia (cat. 44, p. 72). The hand-carved armrests and legs echo the antelope's slender and distinctive soaring horns and sturdy hind legs. The nyala is important to Ethiopian culture and is even featured on the Ethiopian ten-cent coin (fig. 1). It is today considered an endangered species, with fewer than three thousand remaining in Ethiopia's southeastern highlands.

Fig. 1. Ethiopian ten-cent coin.

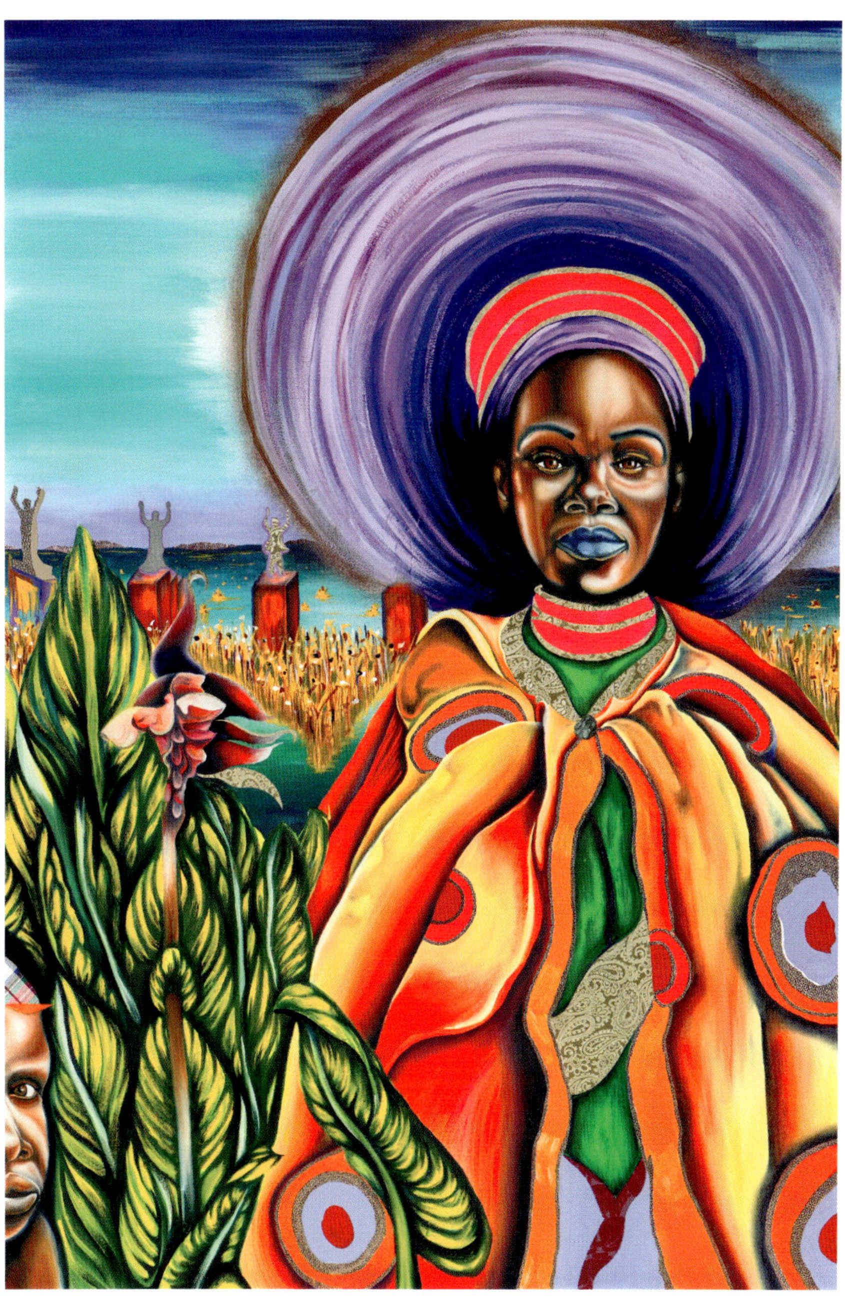

Cat. 43. Phumelele Tshabalala (South African American, born 1987). *A monument to the iS'pantsula as mama feeds the community*, 2021. Mixed media on canvas, 65 × 45 × 3 in. Gift of Jeffrey Magid, 2021.421.

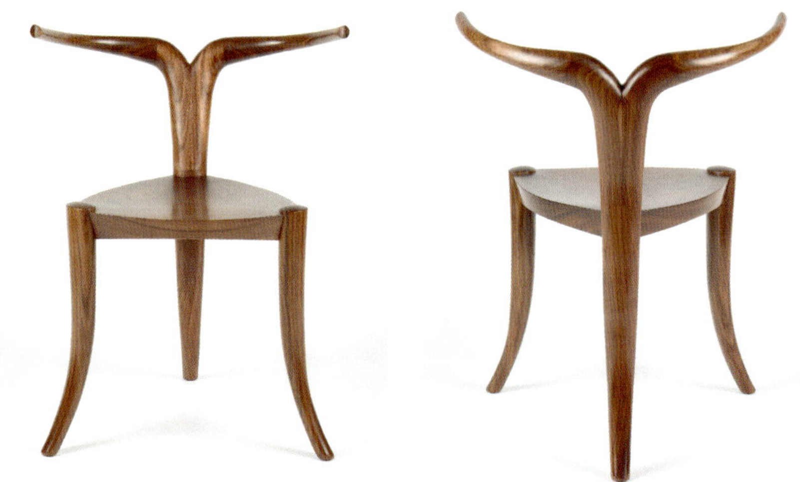

Cat. 44. Jomo Tariku (Ethiopian American, born 1968). *Nyala Chair*, 2017–19. American walnut, 30 × 24 × 20¾ in. Manufactured by David Bohnhoff (American, born 1968). Funds from Gayle and Gary Landis, 2021.392.

For Nifemi Ogunro, a Nigerian American designer and artist based in Brooklyn, her "functional sculptures" reimagine how we have traditionally engaged with furniture. She challenges the assumptions we make about functionality. When talking about her work, she has said, "I want the pieces I make to act as works of art that happen to serve a function. This mindset has allowed me to challenge how a chair, side table, or even a shelf looks and is interacted with."[75] Her work *Nela* echoes the carved headrests from West African cultures that served as status symbols for their owners (cats. 45 and 46). At the same time, because it is a side table, not a stool or headrest, it challenges the ways we build our environments to accommodate our perspectives. Ogunro reminds us that challenges to our usual perspectives for wood carvings is an invitation for growth.

André Griffo is part of the Black diaspora in Brazil. His paintings thoughtfully reflect on the colonial traumas that are integral to the region's identity. They engage with how specific locations—such as subway stations, Renaissance churches, and colonial houses in Brazil—can activate memories in the public's collective consciousness. *Instruções para administração das fazendas 5 (Instructions for the administration of farms 5)* is part of a series in which Griffo represents

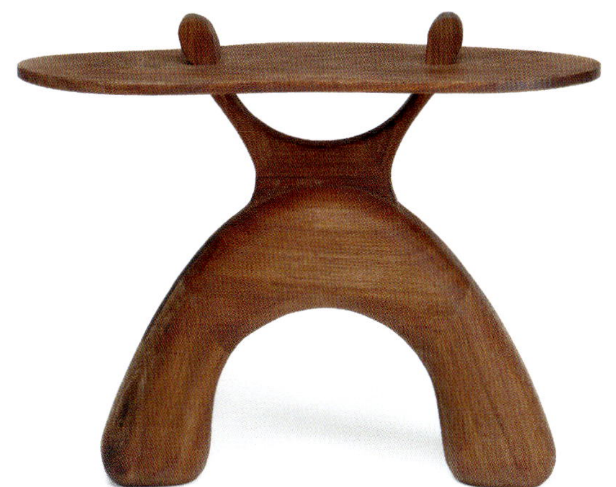

Cat. 45. Nifemi Ogunro (Nigerian American, born 1995). *Nela*, 2022. Walnut, 20⅜ × 26⅛ × 12⅛ in. Funds from Gayle and Gary Landis, 2022.46.

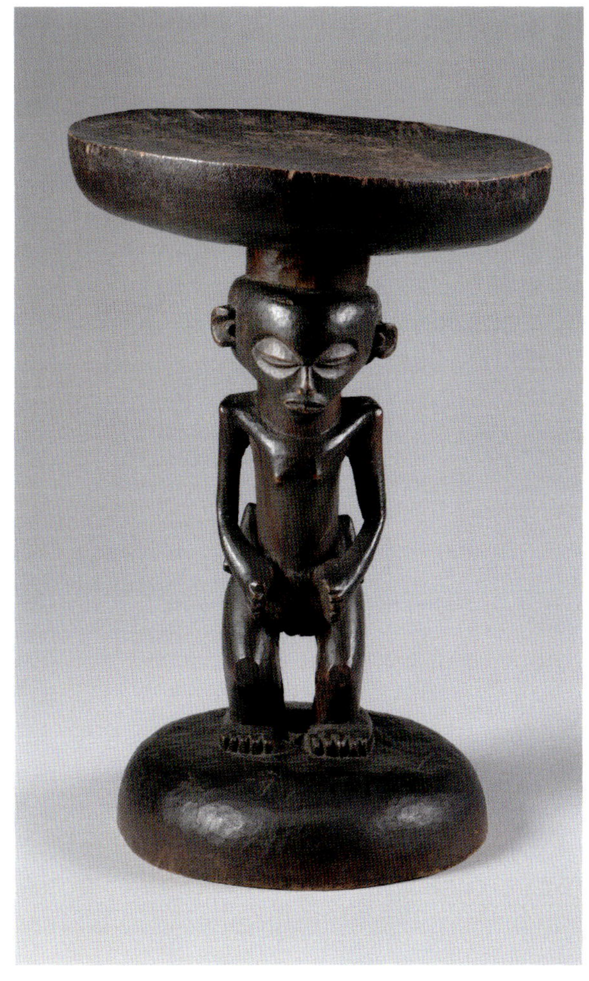

Cat. 46. Chokwe artist. Stool, 1900s. Carved wood, 16⅛ × 11⅛ × 11¼ in. Anonymous gift, 2001.1136.

various views of one of the oldest religious buildings in Rio de Janeiro: the Santa Casa da Misericórdia (Holy House of Mercy), founded in the second half of the sixteenth century (cat. 47). It is the oldest hospital in the city and is still active. Griffo's painting contrasts the hospital's present charitable reputation with haunting reminders of the stolen labor of enslaved peoples who built it by interspersing miniature Black figures at work on a plantation on the floor of the hospital, while paintings of two male colonial masters look down from the walls above, reminding the viewer of how such buildings were funded, built, and maintained.

Fred Wilson, a conceptual artist renowned worldwide for his interdisciplinary practice, makes art that challenges assumptions about history, culture, race, and the conventions of display. By reframing objects and cultural symbols, he alters traditional interpretations, encouraging viewers to reconsider social and historical narratives. In *Untitled (Atlas)*, a plaster cast of the Classical Greek god Atlas, who was doomed to bear the weight of the world on his back, shows how Black artists carry the burden of racial marginalization (cat. 48, p. 76). The piece features the deity weighed down by a stack of art history books that have excluded the work of Black artists, reminding viewers that art-historical biases have shaped notions of beauty and privilege in the Eurocentric world. The figure stands upon a volume devoted to African art, visualising how it is viewed as a footnote in comparison to Western visual culture.

David Huffman calls his paintings "social abstractions." Influenced by progressive Black politics, Afrofuturism, Pop art, basketball, and the television shows *Star Trek* and *Astro Boy*, Huffman combines and mixes references to reflect on the African American experience. *Provo Soul* is inspired by mid-1960s counterculture in Berkeley, California (cat. 49, p. 77). In this painting, basketballs tumble and bound, and the outlines of hoops, next to text, emerge from the dense layers of abstraction. Images of planets transport the viewer to cosmic realms, alongside Huffman's "Traumanauts," Black astronauts who explore the universe in search of origins beyond the constraints of space and time.[76] Huffman's work probes the politics of race within larger systems of exploitation and subjugation, reconciling historical Black trauma with a liberatory horizon.

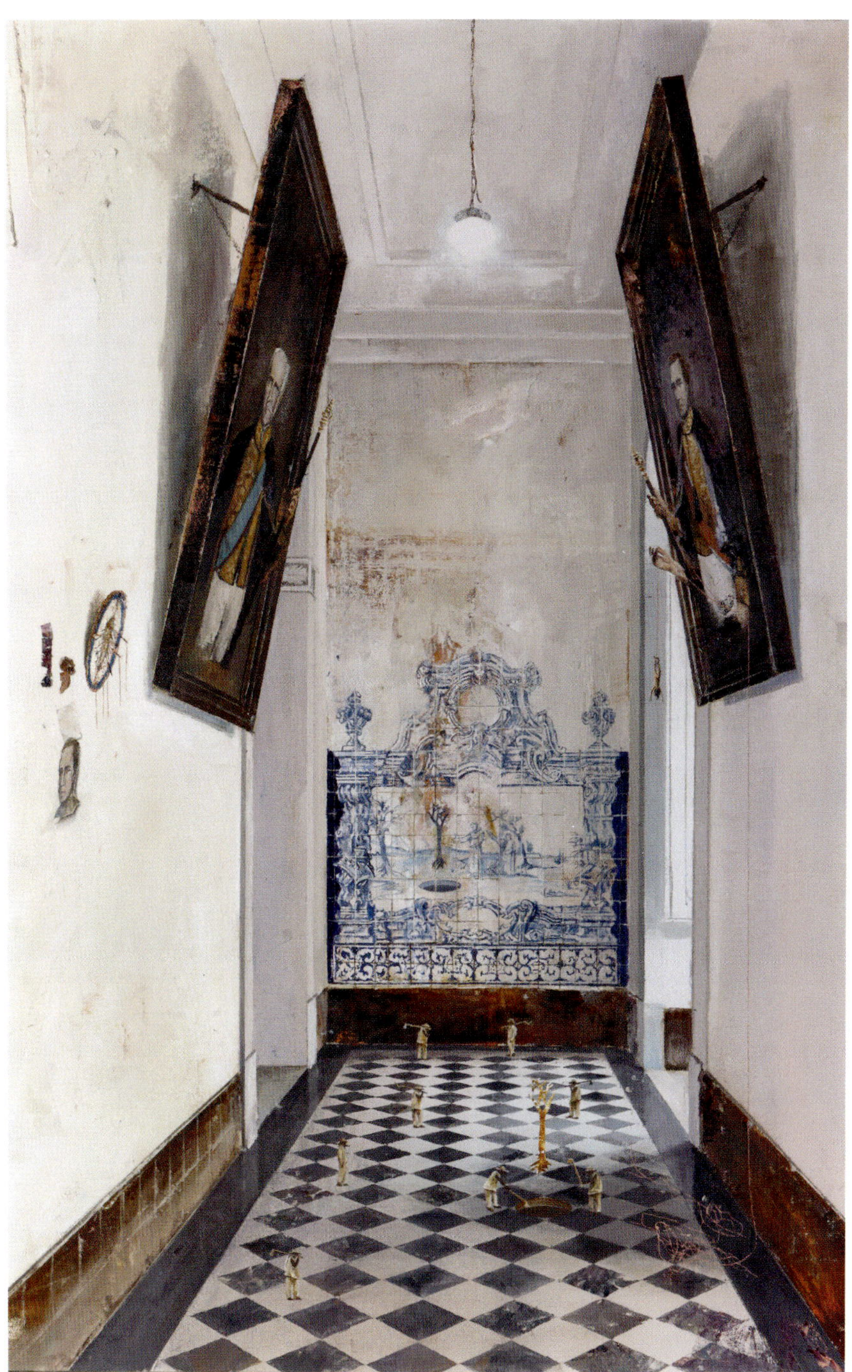

Cat. 47. André Griffo (Brazilian, born 1979). *Instruções para administração das fazendas 5 (Instructions for the administration of farms 5)*, 2021. Oil and acrylic on canvas, 63⅛ × 47⅜ in. Gift of Álvaro Piquet Pessôa, 2021.601.

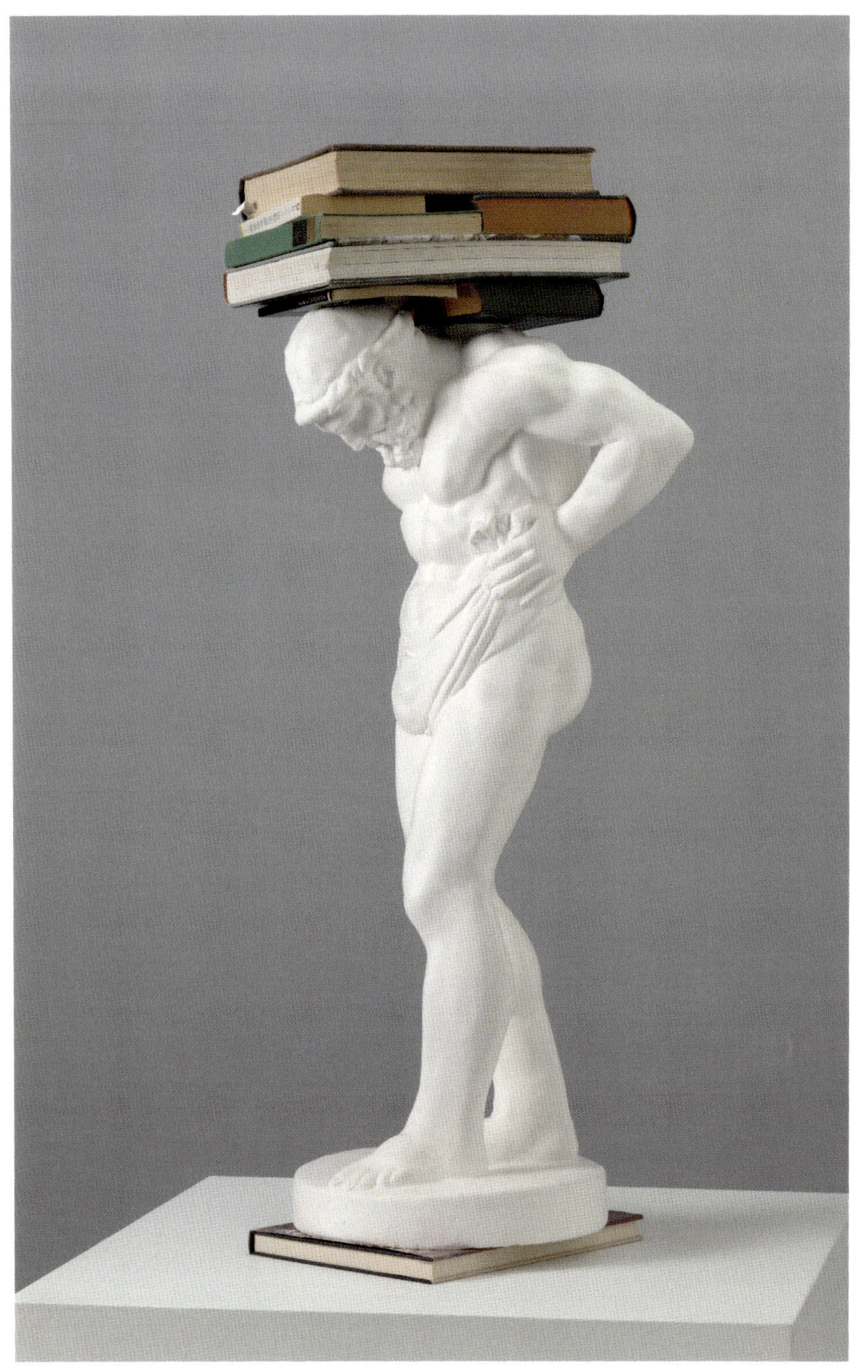

Cat. 48. Fred Wilson (American, born 1954). *Untitled (Atlas)*, 1992. Plaster and books on pedestal, 43 × 16 × 17 in. Funds from Alliance for Contemporary Art and Colorado Contemporary Collectors, 1992.556A-C.

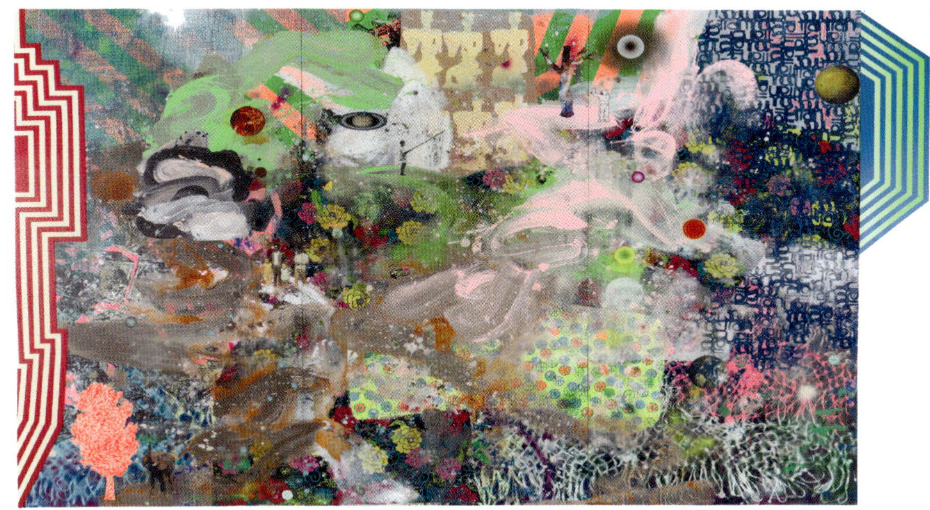

Cat. 49. David Huffman (American, born 1963). *Provo Soul*, 2023. Acrylic, oil, spray paint, African cloth, photo collage, glitter, crayon, and graphite on gesso-coated birch door skin, 96 × 154 in. Funds from Contemporary Collectors' Circle with additional support from Vicki & Kent Logan, Craig Ponzio, Bryon Adinoff & Trish Holland, Kathryn & David Birnbaum, Catherine Dews Edwards & Philip Edwards, and Drs. Ellen & Morris Susman, 2023.399A-D.

Kerry James Marshall's work is also rooted in Black American popular culture and draws upon his own childhood memories and experiences. *Better Homes, Better Gardens* is part of a series of paintings that Marshall calls the *Garden Project* that portrays scenes that suggest the complexity of life in low-income public housing (cat. 50, p. 78). Marshall challenges the negative stereotypes of a housing development by creating a more hopeful scene set against the institutional backdrop—two young people embrace one another as they stroll down a path, bluebirds flutter near the top of the painting, and cheerful sunbeams pop up from behind the building. "What I wanted to show in those paintings is that whatever you think about the projects, they're that and more. If you think they're full of hopelessness and despair, you're wrong. There are actually a lot of opportunities to experience pleasure in the projects."[77]

Denver-born artist Jordan Casteel is also drawn to significant sites in diasporic history, especially Harlem's vibrant street life and arts scene. From the Great Migration north and the arts renaissance of the 1920s, through social unrest, financial hardship, and gentrification, Harlem has been a major Black residential, cultural, and business hub for more than a century.

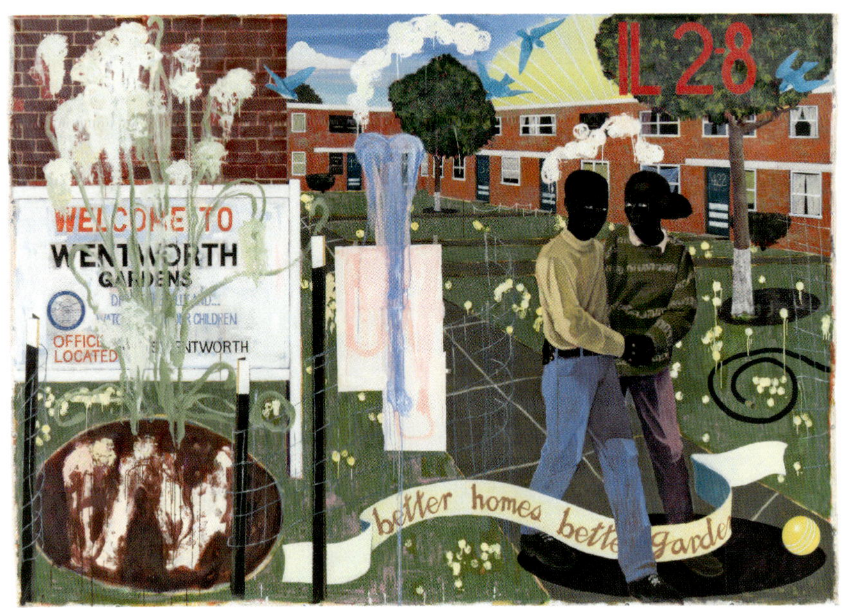

Cat. 50. Kerry James Marshall (American, born 1955). *Better Homes, Better Gardens*, 1994. Acrylic and paper collage on canvas, 100 × 142 in. Funds from Polly and Mark Addison, the Alliance for Contemporary Art, Caroline Morgan, and Colorado Contemporary Collectors: Suzanne Farver, Linda and Ken Heller, Jan and Frederick Mayer, Judy and Ken Robins, Beverly and Bernard Rosen, Annalee and Wagner Schorr, and anonymous donors, 1995.77.

In *Sylvia's (Taniedra, Kendra, Bedelia, Crizette, De'Sean)*, Casteel paints the descendants of Sylvia Woods, seated in the restaurant and looking directly at the viewer, as if sparking a conversation (cat. 51). Sylvia's was opened in the 1950s by Woods and her husband to celebrate African American resilience through authentic soul food. Classic dishes include fried chicken, barbecued ribs, collard greens, potato salad, and cornbread. When speaking about the dynamic between herself and her subjects, Casteel has said, "What does it mean to offer someone visibility in a world that is constantly rendering their humanity invisible? I relinquish a ton of control over how a painting is perceived once it leaves my studio, however, I can and do work really hard to make sure it is full of empathy and respect."[78]

A Global World: Museums and Restitution

Beyond celebrating Black art and artists in resisting erasure, museums have additional responsibilities. The Denver Art Museum is committed to restitutionary work that reshapes cultural relations and forges shared progressive futures amid polarization. In 2022, the museum deaccessioned a Benin bronze plaque that was on view in the Arts of Africa gallery (p. 81). When the museum purchased it in 1955, it was unaware of its complete history. Newly accessible provenance in 2022 showed that the plaque was one of thousands looted in a punitive expedition in 1897 when British soldiers invaded and destroyed the royal palace of the Oba (king) of Benin (present-day Edo State, Nigeria).[79]

The term "Benin bronzes" comes from the many cast-bronze items that once adorned that royal palace. Today, the term collectively refers to exquisitely crafted ivory objects, metal casts, wood carvings, terracotta

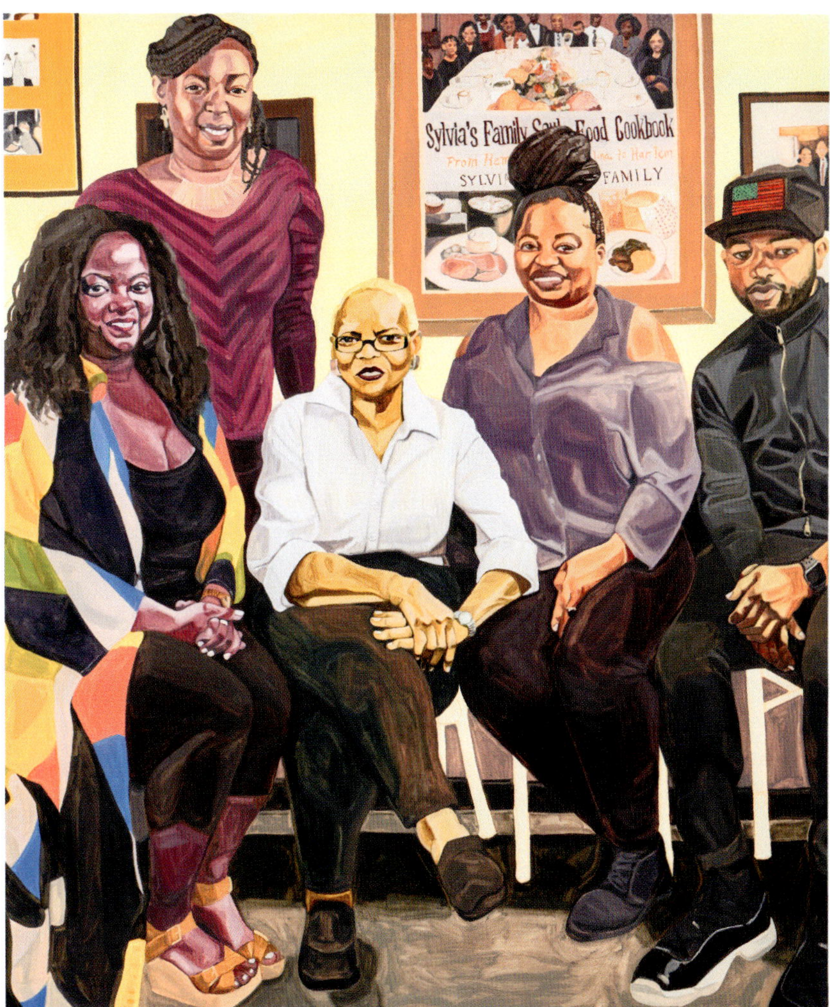

Cat. 51. Jordan Casteel (American, born 1989). *Sylvia's (Taniedra, Kendra, Bedelia, Crizette, De'Sean)*, 2018. Oil paint on canvas, 90 × 78 in. Purchased with funds from CultureHaus, Burgess Services, Maude B. Lofton MD, Robert F. Smith Family, Tina Walls, and Contemporary Alliance, 2019.20.

sculptures, and other artworks commissioned by the Benin royal court.[80] A lesser-known fact about the Benin bronzes is that trade with the Portuguese in the fifteenth and sixteenth centuries likely encouraged the development of brass casting in Benin. Because West Africa did not produce enough metal to supply Benin City's brass-casting industry, trade with merchants from outside Africa filled the gap. The Portuguese arrived in present-day Benin from the Atlantic and traded their brass ingots, often made in the form of bracelets, for pepper, cloth, ivory, and enslaved people.[81] As this publication has shown, African cultures, such as the one in Benin City, never existed in isolation. There was always movement, trade, and the exchange of ideas—and the artwork of the time reflects this.

When the plaque was deaccessioned in 2022, communication was initiated with the rightful owners in Nigeria, the National Commission for Museums and Monuments (NCMM). The museum successfully signed an agreement in April 2025 that allowed a five-year loan of the Benin bronze plaque. In July 2025, the plaque was reinstalled in the arts of Africa gallery, accompanied by an interpretive label that shares this history. Such a partnership with the NCMM also reflects that restitution of African artworks is not just putting things in a crate and shipping them back to the relevant museum or community. Rather, it requires repairing and building new ways of relating that bring to the fore what has been erased, suppressed, and muted.

The restitution of objects represents only one dimension of redress. Another equally vital form of restitution is the redistribution of narrative power through collaborative curatorial practice. If repatriation asks "what must be returned?," co-curation asks the deeper question: "Who has the right to speak for these objects in the first place?" See Margaret Nagawa's investigation into one artwork's history in the sidebar on pgs. 82-83 for a recent example from our collection.

Restitutionary work, therefore, moves along two interconnected trajectories—reversing historical dispossession through returns while simultaneously dismantling the hierarchies of knowledge production that legitimized that dispossession. Beyond the act of return lies the ongoing work of remaking institutional relationships, where communities and people become partners rather than subjects in the interpretation of their own heritage. Ultimately, restitutionary work is central to constructing a shared world that restores humanity, repairs broken links, and relaunches forms of reciprocity necessary for a fully human world for all.

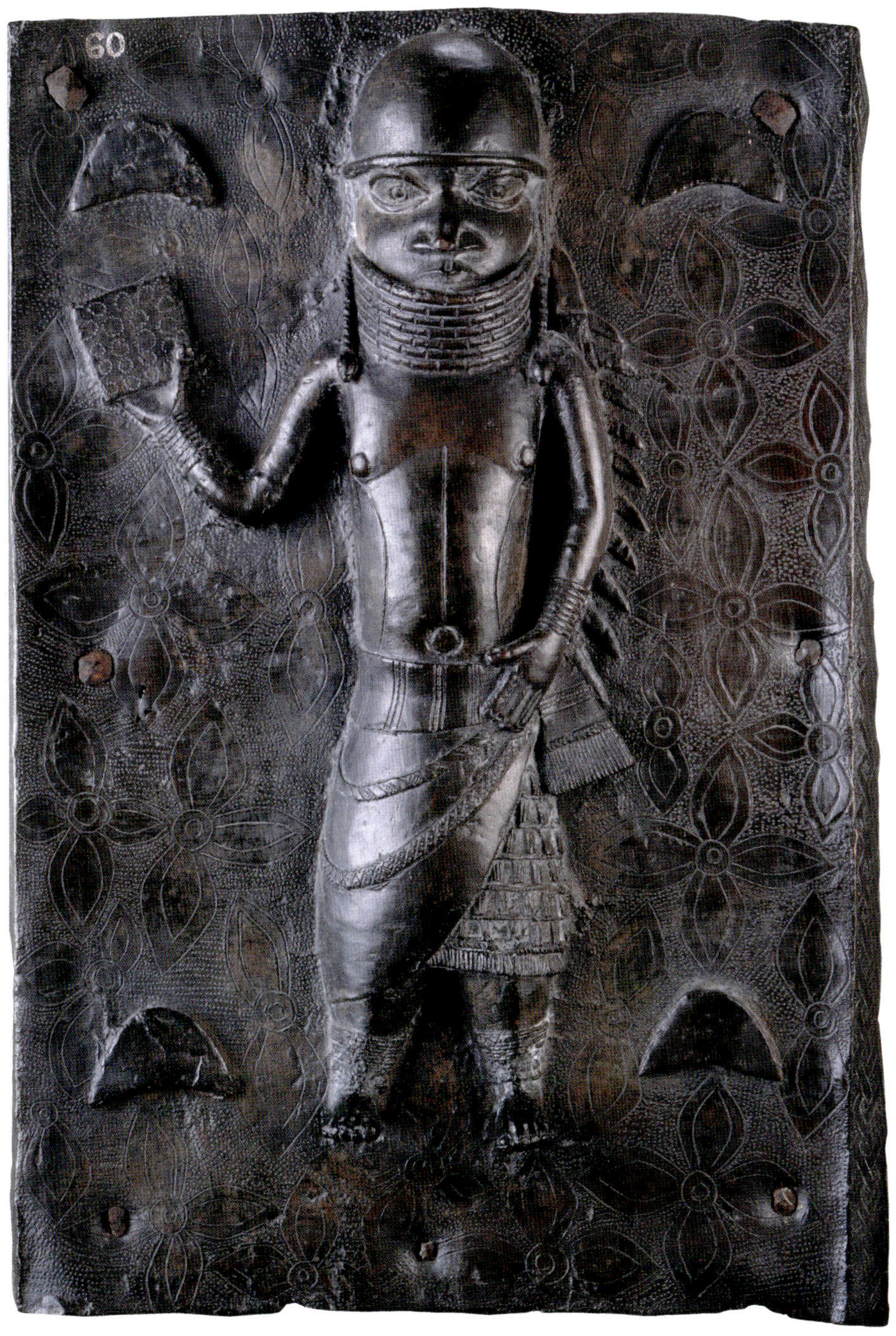

Benin artist. Benin Plaque, 1550–1650. Bronze, 20¼ × 14⅛ in. Work loaned by the National. Commission for Museums and Monuments of Nigeria, 1955.317.2.

PINNING DOWN A DATE: THE PRODUCTION OF FRANCIS NNAGGENDA'S *SPIRITUAL MESSENGER*

Margaret Nagawa

In 2024, the Denver Art Museum website stated that Francis Nnaggenda's sculpture *Spiritual Messenger* was made in the 1970s (cat. 52). Nnaggenda is a sculptor based in Namulanda, Uganda, who creates monumental sculptures in wood and metal, often repurposing materials.[1] The sculpture's production date, ascribed broadly to the 1970s, presented an opportunity to explore historical specificity. I argue that the provenance documentation on file, complemented by conversations with the artist, narrows the window of production dates.

Spiritual Messenger comprises dark-brown metal rods and car parts, bent and welded into a life-size figure with large, protruding eyes. The surface is slightly glossy owing to a wax finish. The hair, rendered as a crisscross pattern of short, welded rods, introduces rhythmic texture and directional movement, and a section of a bright red car body part animates the back of the figure, its scratched surface exposing the steel metal beneath. The tubular base, painted red on the inside, glows from within, suggesting that the work's vitality emanates from its core.

According to the acquisition files, *Spiritual Messenger* entered the collection in 2001 as a gift from Robert and Mary Udall of Fort Collins, Colorado. In a handwritten letter dated September 6, 2001, Mary wrote to Moyo Okediji, then associate curator of African art, "Did I tell you that my husband Robert traded his Citroën sedan to Francis Nnaggenda for the sculpture?" In the same letter, she also stated that her husband left Kenya in 1971, where he had served as faculty in veterinary science at the University of Nairobi since 1965.[2] Nnaggenda also happened to have been a professor at the University of Nairobi from 1968 to 1978. This correspondence places Robert Udall and Francis Nnaggenda in the same country around 1970 or 1971.

However, I was cautious about relying on the memory of one person. On January 24, 2025, Nnaggenda himself confirmed to me that the sculpture was indeed traded for the Citroën in Nairobi. Art historians Susan Elizabeth Gagliardi and Yaëlle Biro have stated, in a different context, that examining the provenance of artworks and acknowledging knowledge gaps can help address unequal power structures.[3] Involving Nnaggenda in the process of recovering his sculpture's history addresses the power imbalance between the institution and the individual artist in writing history and enriches the firsthand information on file.

By correlating museum records with firsthand testimony, *Spiritual Messenger* can be more accurately dated to Nnaggenda's early years in Nairobi, around 1970 or 1971. This tighter chronology situates the work within a verifiable historical and geographic context, underscoring the value of consulting artists in efforts to enhance the accuracy of museum documentation.

[1] See Sunanda K. Sanyal, "The Local and Beyond: Francis Nnaggenda's Sculptural Innovations," *NKA (Brooklyn, N.Y.)* 18, no. 1 (2003): 76–79; and Sidney L. Kasfir, "Nnaggenda: Experimental Ugandan Artist," *African Arts* 3, no. 1 (1969): 8–88, for discussions of Nnaggenda's large-scale sculptures.

[2] "In Memoriam," American Veterinary Medical Association, August 15, 2001, https://www.avma.org/javma-news/2001-09-01/memoriam.

[3] Susan Elizabeth Gagliardi and Yaëlle Biro, "Beyond Single Stories: Addressing Dynamism, Specificity, and Agency in Arts of Africa," *African Arts 52,* no. 4 (2019): 5.

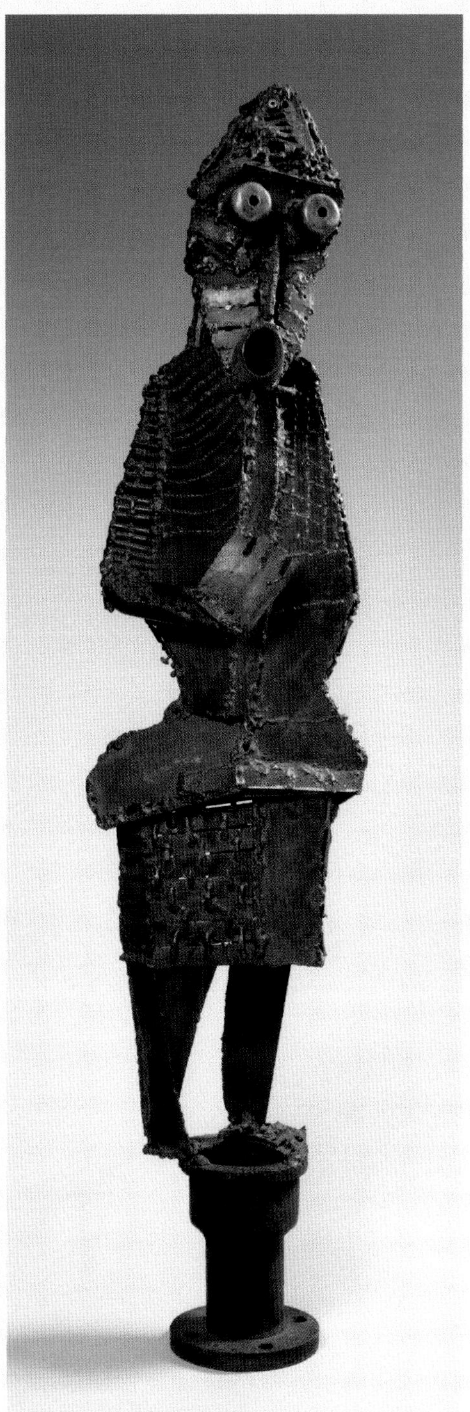

Cat. 52. Francis Nnaggenda (Ugandan, born 1936). *Spiritual Messenger*, 1970–71.
Metal, 58½ × 13 × 13 in.
Gift of Robert and Mary Udall, 2001.644.

ENDNOTES

[1] Babatunde Lawal, "Èjìwàpò: The Dialectics of Twoness in Yoruba Art and Culture," African Arts 41, no. 1 (2008): 24–39.

[2] Kathleen Bickford Berzock, ed. *Caravans of Gold, Fragments in Time: Art, Culture, and Exchange Across Medieval Saharan Africa,* (Block Museum of Art, Northwestern University, Princeton University Press, 2019), 189.

[3] Sandy Prita Meier, *Swahili Port Cities: The Architecture of Elsewhere* (Indiana University Press, 2016), 19.

[4] Francis B. Nyamnjoh, "Rethinking Citizenship in 21st Century Africa: Some Conceptual Considerations," in *Citizenship in Motion: South African and Japanese Scholars in Conversation*, ed. Itsuhiro Hazama, Kiyoshi Umeya, and Francis B. Nyamnjoh (Langaa Research and Publishing Group and The Center for African Area Studies, Kyoto University), 401–16.

[5] Berzock, *Caravans of Gold, Fragments in Time*, 181.

[6] Ibid, 184.

[7] National Geographic Society, "Mansa Musa (Musa I of Mali)," National Geographic online encyclopedia entry, October 19, 2023, https://education.nationalgeographic.org/resource/mansa-musa-musa-i-mali/.

[8] Christina Griffith, "The Asante Gold Weights: Practical, Unique, Artistic Tools of the Trade," *Expedition Magazine* 61, no. 2 (2019), https://www.penn.museum/sites/expedition/the-asante-gold-weights/.

[9] Timothy F. Garrard, *Akan Weights and the Gold Trade* (Longman, 1980), 173.

[10] Griffith, "The Asante Gold Weights."

[11] Ibid.

[12] Kwame Anthony Appiah, "The Arts of Africa," *New York Review*, April 24, 1997, https://www.nybooks.com/articles/1997/04/24/the-arts-of-africa/.

[13] Garrard, *Akan Weights and the Gold Trade*, 173.

[14] Eivind Heldaas Seland, "The Periplus of the Erythraean Sea: A Network Approach," *Asian Review of World Histories* 4, no. 2 (2016): 191–205.

[15] Dionisius Grandy Fharose, "The Crown of a Man: Muslim Skullcaps, Modernity, and Belonging in the Nineteenth–Twentieth-Century Indian Ocean World," *Journal of Indian Ocean World Studies* 8, no. 2 (2024): 103–26, https://muse.jhu.edu/article/957241.

[16] Meier, *Swahili Port Cities*, 8.

[17] Shiela Unwin, "The Origins and Categories of 'Arab' Chests: With Particular Reference to Oman," *Proceedings of the Seminar for Arabian Studies* 18 (1988): 155–61, http://www.jstor.org/stable/41223074.

[18] Ibid.

[19] Meier, *Swahili Port Cities*, 19.

[20] Jean-Baptiste Bacquart, *The Tribal Arts of Africa* (Thames and Hudson, 1998), 108.

[21] Kathy Curnow, *Bright Continent: African Art History*, 2nd ed. (MSL Academic Endeavors eBooks, 2021), 23, https://engagedscholarship.csuohio.edu/msl_ae_ebooks/23.

[22] Sidney Littlefield Kasfir, *Contemporary African Art*, 2nd ed. (Thames and Hudson, 2020), 104.

[23] Jean Michel Massing and Joana Danimbe, *Sensibilités Vaudou dans l'art contemporain d'Afrique* (Fondation Blachère, 2025).

[24] Joanne B. Eicher and Doran Ross, ed., *Berg Encyclopedia of World Dress and Fashion Volume 1: Africa* (Berg Publishers, 2011), 120.

[25] Daniela Calvo, "Harm in Yoruba Cosmology — The Ajogun as Active Forces Contributing to Cosmic and Social Order," *Axis Mundi* 17, no. 2 (2022): 13–22, https://fphil.uniba.sk/fileadmin/fif/katedry_pracoviska/kpr/axismundi/Axis_Mundi_2_2022-16-10-fin-web-14-22_Calvo.pdf

[26] *Sensibilités Vaudou dans l'art contemporain d'Afrique* by Jean Michel Massing and Joana Danimbe, pg. 37 27 Calvo, "Harm in Yoruba Cosmology," 13–22.

[27] 27 Calvo, "Harm in Yoruba Cosmology," 13–22.

[28] Ibid.

[29] Lawal, "Èjìwàpò," 24–39.

[30] Ibid.

[31]Ayodele Ogundipe, *Ẹ̀ṣù Elégbára, Chance, Uncertainty in Yorùbá Mythology*, 2 vols. (Indiana University, 1978), 1:3.

[32] Ibid., 1:4

[33] Massing and Danimbe, *Sensibilités Vaudou dans l'art contemporain d'Afrique*, 37.

[34] Lawal, "Èjìwàpò," 24–39.

[35] Edna G. Bay, *Asen, Ancestors, and Vodun: Tracing Change in African Art* (University of Illinois Press, 2008), 30.

[36] Ade Dopamu, "The Yoruba Religious System," Africa Update 6, no. 3 (1999): 2–17.

[37] Massing and Danimbe, *Sensibilités Vaudou dans l'art contemporain d'Afrique*, 37.

[38] Kọ́láz Abímbọ́lá, *Yoruba Culture: A Philosophical Account*, 1st ed. (Iroko Academic Publishers, 2005), 27.

[39] Ibid.

[40] Ibid.

[41] Bacquart, *The Tribal Arts of Africa*, 100.

[42] Ibid.

[43] Ibid.

[44] Fernand Leroy, Taiwo Olaleye-Oruene, Gesina Koeppen-Schomerus, and Elizabeth Bryan, "Yoruba Customs and Beliefs Pertaining to Twins," *Twin Research* 5, no. 2 (2002): 134.

[45] Ibid.

[46] Bacquart, *The Tribal Arts of Africa*, 100.

[47] Ibid., 103.

[48] Victor Ikechukwu Ukaegbu, "The Composite Scene: The Aesthetics of Igbo Mask Theatre" (PhD diss., University of Plymouth, 1996), 35.

[49] Lasbrey Ikechukwu Unegbu and Anayo Maxwell Onanwa, "Socio-Longustic Inquiry on Okoroshi Language," *Journal of Nigeria Languages' Studies* 8, no. 1 (2024): 51–57.

[50] Peri Klemm, Steven Zucker, and Christa Clark, "Bundu/Sowei Helmet Mask (Mende People)," Smarthistory, November 12, 2015, https://smarthistory.org/bundu-sowei-helmet-mask/.

[51] Annelies Hickendorff, *Gabon: The Bradt Travel Guide* (Bradt Travel Guides, 2014), 21.

[52] Africa Direct, "The Influence of African Art on Modern Artists and Design," March 1, 2025, https://africadirect.com/blogs/news/the-influence-of-african-art-on-modern-artists-and-design?srsltid=AfmBOopxl-raxKs-X0GTTpcHIG76mdyuZscYap4VtnEvw-ci677dbhhm42.

[53] Louis Perrois and Pierre-Alain Ferrazzini, *Ancestral Art of Gabon: From the Collections of the Barbier-Mueller Museum* (Barbier-Mueller Museum, 1985), 100.

[54] Ayodeji Olukoju, *Culture and Customs of Liberia* (Greenwood Press, 2006), 37.

[55] Susan Mullin Vogel, *Baule: African Art, Western Eyes* (Yale University Art Gallery and Yale University Press, 1997), 101.

[56] Randy P. Conner, "Sexuality and Gender in African Spiritual Traditions," in *Sexuality and the World's Religions*, ed. David W. Machacek and Melissa M. Wilcox (ABC-CLIO, 2003), 3–30.

[57] Frederick Lamp, "Art of the Baga: A Drama of Cultural Reinvention," *African Arts*, 29, no. 4 (1996): 20–33.

[58] Kasfir, *Contemporary African Art*, 111.

[59] Jennifer Miller March, "Why We Must Challenge the Typical Museum Narrative Regarding Ancient Egypt," *Hyperallergic*, March 29, 2022, https://hyperallergic.com/720391/why-we-must-challenge-the-typical-museum-narrative-regarding-ancient-egypt/.

[60] Ibid.

[61] "Dogon Mask," Timothy S. Y. Lam Museum of Anthropology, accessed November 19, 2025, https://lammuseum.wfu.edu/2020/07/dogon-mask/.

[62] "Simi (Knife Favoured by the Kikuyu Tribe of Kenya)," Imperial War Museums, accessed November 19, 2025.

[63] Naaborko Sackeyfio-Lenoch, Connecting Decolonization in Africa and the US Civil Rights Movement (World History Project, Bill Gates Foundation, 2020).

[64] Kasfir, *Contemporary African Art*, 144.

[65] Ibid, 147.

[66] Ibid.

[67] Ibid.

[68] Ibid, 16.

[69] Allison Young, "El Anatsui, *Old Man's Cloth*," Smarthistory, August 9, 2015, https://smarthistory.org/el-anatsui-old-mans-cloth/.

[70] Simphiwe Ndzube, in Rebecca R. Hart, "Introduction," *Simphiwe Ndzube: Oracles of the Pink Universe* (Denver Art Museum, 2021), 12.

[71] Simphiwe Ndzube, "Sneak Peak of *Simphiwe Ndzube: Oracles of the Pink Universe*, video, Denver Art Museum, 2021, https://www.simphiwendzube.com/oracles-of-the-pink-universe.

[72] Tandazani Dhlakama, "The Everyday: Seeing Ourselves," in *When We See Us: A Century of Black Figuration in Painting*, ed. Tandazani Dhlakama (Thames and Hudson, 2022), 16.

[73] Achille Mbembe, *Critique of Black Reason*, transl. Laurent Duboois (Duke University Press, 2017), 82.

[74] Dhlakama, "The Everyday," 16.

[75] Mollie E. Barnes, "NIFEMI OGUNRO @ BLONDER.THAN.NECESSARY," She Curates, 2020, https://www.she-curates.com/interviews/artists/nifemi-ogunro/

[76] Victoria Sung, "Berkeley Artist David Huffman's New Show Pays Tribute to His Activist Mother," *Berkeleyside*, August 13, 2021, https://www.berkeleyside.org/2021/08/13/david-huffman-berkeley-art-center.

[77] Calvin Reid, interview with Kerry James Marshall, *Bomb* (January 1, 1998), https://bombmagazine.org/articles/1998/01/01/kerry-james-marshall/.

[78] Leah Melby Clinton, "Jordan Casteel on the Power of Art Right Now," *Elle Magazine*, 2017, https://www.elle.com/life-love/a43770/jordan-casteel-artist-interview/.

[79] Dan Hicks, *The Brutish Museums: The Benin Bronzes, Colonial Violence and Cultural Restitution* (Pluto Press, 2020), 249.

[80] "The Historic Trade Between West Africa and Portugal," National Museums Scotland, accessed November 19, 2025, https://www.nms.ac.uk/discover-catalogue/the-historic-trade-btween-west-africa-and-portugal#:~:text=He%20was%20able%20to%20purchase,brass%20currency %20bracelets%20called%20manillas.

[81] Hicks, *The Brutish Museums*, 8.

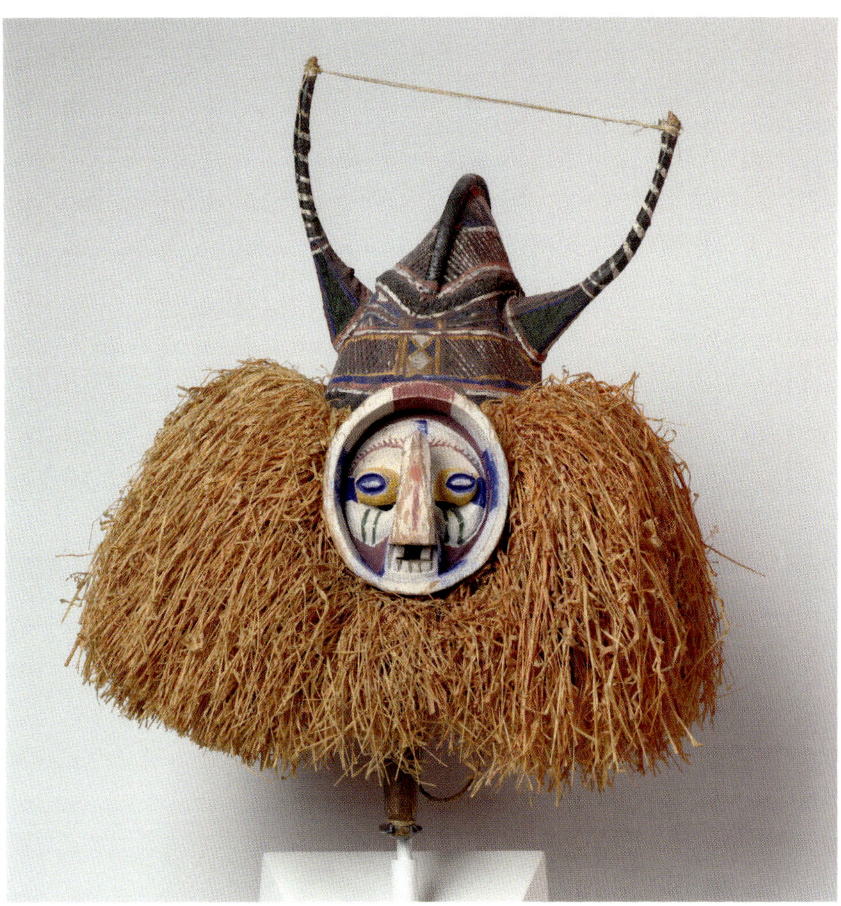

Yaka artist. Kholuka Mask, late 1800s. Wood, plant fiber, and cloth, 20 × 23 × 21 in. Native Arts acquisition funds, 1957.207.

CONTRIBUTING AUTHORS

Merikokeb Berhanu is an Ethiopian artist based in Maryland.

Syokau Mutonga is the Anderman Family Fellow for Arts of Africa at the Denver Art Museum.

Margaret Nagawa is a curator and a PhD student focused on contemporary African art in the art history department at Emory University, Atlanta.

Kendall Taylor is an African Americanist who studied at Metropolitan State University of Denver and West Virginia University.

IMAGE CREDITS

pp. 4–5; p. 7; p. 12, cat. 2; p. 13, cats. 3–4; pp. 14–15; p. 17, cat. 5; p. 19, cat. 7; p. 26, cat. 12; p. 27, cat. 13; p. 28; p. 29, cat. 14; p. 38, cat. 22; p. 47, cat. 29; p. 60, cat. 35; p. 64, cat. 39; p. 69, cat. 42; p. 71, cat. 43; p. 72, cat. 44; p. 73, cat. 45; p. 81, cat. 96; p. 83, cat. 52: **Photos by Christina Jackson, courtesy Denver Art Museum**

p. 10, cat. 1; p. 21, cat. 9; p. 22, cat. 10; p. 31, cats. 15–16; p. 35, cat. 17; p. 35, cats. 19–20; p. 37, cat. 21; p. 39, cat. 23; p. 40, cat. 24; p. 41, cat. 25; p. 45, cat. 28; p. 50, cat. 32; p. 54, lower left; p. 55, top row and lower left; p. 56, top right; p. 57; p. 62, cat. 37; p. 63, cat. 38; p. 66, cat. 40; p. 75, cat. 47; p. 76, cat. 48; p. 77, cat 49: **Photos by Bruce Fernandez, courtesy Denver Art Museum**

p. 19, cat. 6; p. 20, cat. 8; p. 23, cat. 11; p. 42, cat. 26; p. 48, cat. 30; p. 49, cat. 31, p. 54, top row; p. 55; p. 56, top left and lower left; p. 73, cat. 46: **Photos by Eric Stephenson, courtesy Denver Art Museum**

p. 34, cat. 18: **Photo by Jane Johnson, courtesy Denver Art Museum**

p. 44, cat. 27; p. 59, cat. 34; p. 68, cat. 41; p. 78, cat. 50: **Photos by Jeff Wells, courtesy Denver Art Museum**

p. 52, fig. 1: **© Thomas Jefferson University**

p. 53, cat. 33: **Photo by Kevin Hester, courtesy Denver Art Museum**

p. 59, cat. 34: **© El Anatsui**

p. 60, cat. 35: **© Simphiwe Ndzube**

p. 61, cat. 36: **© Alioune Diagne. Photography courtesy the artist and TEMPLON, Paris–Brussels–NYC. © Isabelle Arthuis**

p. 62, cat. 37: **© Cheick Diallo**

p. 63, cat. 38: **© 2022 Studio Hamed Ouattara, All rights reserved**

p. 64, cat. 39: **© Andile Dyalvane**

p. 66, cat. 40: **© Merikokeb Berhanu**

p. 70, fig. 1: **© Katz Coins Notes & Supplies Corp. (https://en.numista.com/40353)**

p. 71, cat. 43: **© Phumelele Tshabalala**

p. 72, cat. 44: **© Jomo Tariku**

p. 73, cat. 45: **© Nifemi Ogunro**

p. 75, cat. 47: **© André Griffo**

p. 76, cat. 48: **© Fred Wilson**

p. 77, cat. 49: **© David Huffman**

p. 78, cat. 50: **© Kerry James Marshall**

p. 79, cat. 51: **© Jordan Casteel. Image courtesy of the artist and Casey Caplan, New York**

DENVER art MUSEUM

Denver Art Museum
100 West 14th Avenue Parkway
Denver, CO 80204
denverartmuseum.org

The Denver Art Museum is located on the homeland of the Arapaho, Cheyenne, and Ute people, along with many people from other Indigenous nations that call this place home. Learn more about our commitments to better represent, elevate, and support Indigenous cultures and people, past and present, on our website.

ISBN 978-1-945483-22-6

Library of Congress Control Number: 2026930468

Project Manager: Leslie Murrell
Managing Editor: Valerie Hellstein
Curatorial Assistant: Caitlin O'Beirne
Manager of Rights and Reproductions: Renée B. Miller
Book design: Mary Junda
Printing: Shapco Printing, Minneapolis

Cover, p. 59: Cat. 34. El Anatsui (Ghanaian, Ewe culture, born 1944). *Rain Has No Father?*, 2008. Found bottle tops and copper wire, 153 × 239 in. Funds from Native Arts acquisition funds, U.S. Bank, Richard and Theresa Davis, Douglas Society, Denver Art Museum Volunteer Endowment, Alex Cranberg and Susan Morris, Geta and Janice Asfaw, Saron and Daniel Yohannes, Lee McIntire, Milroy and Sheryl Alexander, Dorothy and Richard Campbell, Wayne Carey and Olivia Thompson, Morris Clark, Rebecca H. Cordes, Kenneth and Rebecca Gart, Tim and Bobbi Hamill, Kalleen and Robert Malone, Meyer and Geri Saltzman, Ann and Gerry Saul, Mary Ellen and Thomas Williams, Nancy and James Williams, Forrest Cason, First Western Trust Bank, Howard and Sandy Gelt, Gene Osborne, Boettcher Foundation, John and Eve Glesne, The Schlegel White Foundation, Jeffrey and Nancy Balter, and Tamara Banks, 2008.891. © El Anatsui

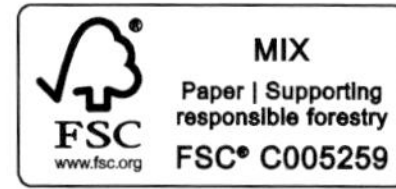